The Sinking of the *Laconia* and the U-Boat War

The Sinking of
the *Laconia* and the
U-Boat War

Disaster in the Mid-Atlantic

JAMES P. DUFFY

University of Nebraska Press
Lincoln and London

The Sinking of the Laconia *and the U-Boat War: Disaster in the Mid-Atlantic*, by James P. Duffy, was originally published in hard cover by Praeger, an imprint of ABC-CLIO, LLC, Santa Barbara, CA. Copyright © 2009 by James P. Duffy. Paperback edition by arrangement with ABC-CLIO, LLC, Santa Barbara, CA. All rights reserved.

Manufactured in the United States of America

First Nebraska paperback printing: 2013

Library of Congress Cataloging-in-Publication Data
Duffy, James P., 1941–
The sinking of the Laconia and the U-boat war: disaster in the Mid-Atlantic /
James P. Duffy.
pages cm
Originally published: Santa Barbara, California: Praeger/ABC-CLIO, 2009.
Includes bibliographical references and index.
ISBN 978-0-8032-4540-2 (paper: alkaline paper) 1. Laconia (Steamship: 1921–1942)
2. Steamboat disasters—Atlantic Ocean—History—20th century. 3. World War, 1939–
1945—Naval operations, German. 4. Submarines (Ships)—Germany—History—20th
century. 5. World War, 1939–1945—Naval operations—Submarine. I. Title.
D772.L23D84 2013
940.54'293—dc23   2012044353

For Iris

"The only thing that ever really frightened me during the war was the U-Boat peril."

—Winston S. Churchill

Contents

A photo essay follows page 62

Acknowledgments

When I first began the research that would lead to the writing of this book, I intended to write solely about the sinking of the *Laconia* and the rescue efforts that followed. However, I discovered that story has been told quite well by a number of authors over the years, some of whom had been passengers on the *Laconia*. It soon became apparent that there was a larger tale that needed to be told—one involving many U-boat commanders, not simply Werner Hartenstein and his comrades of the Laconia Incident. It is that larger story that led to this book.

During the course of writing this book so many people helped in so many ways, great and small, that it became impossible to keep track of their names for inclusion here. The following contributed in one way or another to this book. The list is in no way complete, so I want to say in advance that I appreciate the assistance by everyone during the research and writing of this book.

First, I want to express my appreciation and high regard for Gudmundur Helgason who from his headquarters in Iceland operates the most incredible Web site dealing with U-boats and the U-boat war (http://www.uboat. net). It is the first place to turn for anyone seeking information on those subjects. All the sites I used for research are listed in the Bibliography, including several other fine U-boat sites. An excellent site that deals with the larger picture of the war in the South Atlantic, where much U-boat action took place, is http://sixtant.net, from Ozires Moraes, who resides on the Brazilian coast looking out on that ocean.

Then there is a sort of general "thank you" to the members who participate in several online forums and discussion groups who responded so diligently to my many questions about specific details. These include the forums on u-boat.net, ubootwaffe.net, and H-War.

A personal thanks once again goes to the following: Jean Hood, author of several excellent books herself; Jak Mallmann Showell, another fine author who specializes in naval and submarine topics and was instrumental in introducing me to Horst Bredow at the Deutsches U-Boat Museum-Archive and facilitated my photograph search. The museum's American representative, Guy Goodboe, also helped me with this. Don Gray, editor of the U156/U-502 Roundtable Newsletter was most helpful, as were the other members of his roundtable, with special recognition to Stan Norcom and Ray Burson. All of the following helped in so many ways: Cristiano D'Adamo; Martina Caspers of the Bundesarchiv; Dick Boyle; Ken Dunn; Holly Reed of the National Archives and Records Administration; Allan Janus of the National Air and Space Museum; Pam Riding of the Huddersfield Library; Mrs. Barbara C. Derych; Ann Snow; Hans Mair; and Sir Lawson.

To the many others who helped me along the way but whose names do not appear above, please once again accept my gratitude for your assistance and my apology for the absence of your name.

Finally, another big thank you to my wife Kathy, whose patience, understanding, and hard work make researching and writing books that interest me possible.

CHAPTER 1

Sighting *Laconia*

When the German submarine commander first caught sight of the excessive amount of dark, dense smoke pouring from the single funnel on the horizon, he was about 900 miles south-southwest of Freetown, Sierra Leone, on the bulging West African coast in the South Atlantic. He was also some 250 miles north-northeast of the secret American air base on Ascension Island. The submarine, known to the Allies as a U-boat, an abbreviated Anglicized version of the German *Unterseeboot*, was near the Equator, running some five degrees from that international imaginary reference line that encircles the globe and divides it into the Northern and Southern Hemispheres. Its destination was Cape Town, on the southern tip of the African continent.

The smoke was first spotted a few minutes after 9:30 in the morning. The weather had been unusually warm and sunny for the past few days, and on this day was expected more of the same. The sky above them was a clear blue with only a few scattered clouds drifting along aimlessly. Even the ocean cooperated with the German hunter, with reduced swells and relatively calm waters. The ship, heading west-northwest at a considerable speed, was at a far distance and it would take at least several hours to bring the vessel within range of the submarine's torpedoes.

Following the instructions issued to all U-boat commanders, the submarine took plenty of time to close with the suspect vessel, which after all might not be an enemy vessel, or even one that was worth the firing of one or two of the submarine's precious torpedoes. Admiral Karl Donitz, commander of the U-boat fleets, had instructed his submarine commanders to attack at night while on the surface whenever the option presented itself. He did not want them to attack a ship while submerged, since that reduced the sub's speed and its chances of a successful strike at its target.

At night, a surfaced U-boat was nearly invisible to lookouts aboard a moving ship. Additionally, a daylight attack on an enemy ship exposed the U-boat to the possibility that the target was actually the bait in a trap, and the sky would suddenly be filled with enemy aircraft.

CHAPTER 2

U-Boats at War

Imagine this: Several torpedoes have hit a cargo ship. The vessel is ablaze, lighting the warm night sky with blistering red and orange flames that climb high into the darkness. The deafening racket created by the constant explosions and the roiling sea as the huge ship rocks from side to side, preparing to plunge into the depths, form a terrifying background chorus to the screams of men leaping from the doomed ship into the ocean far below.

As the seawater invades the ship's broken hull and crashes against the large, hot boilers inside, great billows of steam rise around the dying vessel. They carry with them a startling piercing hiss that sounds to those watching from the water in disbelief like the ship's last cry for help. To many of the men who had sailed on her she had been a living thing they had cared for, and now she was dying before their eyes.

While her crew struggles to get away from her, she fills the night with the screeching of metal crashing and rubbing against metal. Her bow suddenly turns down into the ocean, her stern rises out of the water with her single prop still turning, and she quickly vanishes from sight.

As suddenly as the first explosion broke the quiet night, the silence resumes. With the ship gone, the fuel fires burn themselves out. The stillness is broken only by the sounds of voices. Some call for help while others call out the names of shipmates and friends. Who has survived and who has been lost?

The surface of the ocean is littered with debris and survivors from among the ship's several dozen crew members. Many of the wooden lifeboats were shattered in the explosions and their broken pieces now serve as the last hope for the men clinging to them. A few lifeboats endured the disaster but are now overloaded with survivors, and more survivors soaked with seawater and fuel oil hang off their sides. Death is all around them, floating facedown just below the surface. Unspoken, but in every man's mind, is the fear that the noise and the bodies will soon attract that greatest of all predators—sharks.

Suddenly there is a crash of water as a black shadow rises out of the depths nearby. The fear of drowning and of sharks by the dozens is now overcome by a new fear: The U-boat that sunk their ship has surfaced. The hatch on the submarine is thrust open with a bang and Nazi sailors leap out onto the sub's deck and rush to their guns in preparation for the coming slaughter. At the top of the sub's bridge, an arrogant, aristocratic, Aryan-looking German officer gazes out at the chaos he has created with his torpedoes. He is the U-boat's commander. He turns to his gun crews and shouts an order. They respond by opening fire on the cargo ship's survivors in the water and on the lifeboats. When the shooting ceases, the water no longer contains living men, just their bullet-riddled corpses. Soon the bodies and debris will be gone, consumed by the sea and its creatures, and there will be no trace of the U-boat's strike.

Joking and laughing, the German crew descends back into the submarine and the boat slips back beneath the surface and vanishes as quickly as it appeared.

The scene should be rather easy for most readers to envision, for many have witnessed this horrible act of inhumanity before through the fiction of film. As recently as the award-winning 2000 film *U-571*, starring Matthew McConaughey, a U-boat captain is portrayed ordering the execution of a group of unarmed survivors in a lifeboat. The crew appears somewhat disturbed by the order, but they carry out the killings as instructed.

The problem with this and similar scenes from other motion pictures, including Humphrey Bogart's 1943 classic, *Action in the North Atlantic*, is they are not supported by the known facts, with the exception of one documented case. For the commanders and crews of U-boats, killing those who had abandoned ship and were in the water or huddled unarmed in a lifeboat would be tantamount to shooting those who had dropped their weapons and surrendered.

In *Action in the North Atlantic*, not only does the U-boat slice Bogart's lifeboat in half, but an officer on board the submarine films the entire act. This movie might be excused because it was made during the war, and Allied propaganda was spreading fear among merchant seamen and hatred among civilian populations by implying that U-boats routinely killed survivors of the ships they had sunk. There is no excuse for the writers or the director of *U-571* to continue that mischaracterization of U-boat sailors 55 years after the war ended. There were many more instances of the false portrayal of U-boat sailors, even long after Germany surrendered. In 1971's *Murphy's War*, Peter O'Toole seeks revenge on a U-boat skipper for his purposeless machine-gunning of O'Toole's fellow survivors from a sunken ship.

According to Dr. Lawrence H. Suid, a noted historian and author on the relationship between the military and the film industry, the Office of War Information (a U.S. government propaganda agency) issued orders in late 1943 that the portrayal of enemy atrocities in films would no longer be tolerated. In addition, movies containing such scenes would not be given export licenses. This was probably prompted by the realization that the war was going to be won by the Allies, and that we would soon face a new enemy in the expanding and increasingly hostile Soviet Union of Josef Stalin and would require rehabilitated Germany and Japan as allies.

One result of this new policy may have been Alfred Hitchcock's *Lifeboat*, released in 1944. In this film, surviving passengers from a sunken ship, with their diverse backgrounds, are thrown together in a lifeboat, along with the captain of the U-boat who had torpedoed their ship. The U-boat had been sunk in the battle with the ship. The German proves to be the "most practical and most interesting character" on the boat, according to Dr. Suid.

U-boat actions against Allied shipping were governed by the following instructions as entered in the German Naval Staff War Diary, dated October 4, 1939:

Against enemy merchant ships which are known beyond any doubt to be armed or, as the case may be, whose armaments is known through unimpeachable sources of information from the SK1, submarines can make immediate and full use of their weapons. As far as circumstances permit, measures are to be taken for the rescue of the crews after eliminating possible dangers to the submarine. Passenger boats, which are not serving as troop transports, are not, now as before, to be attacked, even when they are armed.

During the Second World War, Germany deployed 806 U-boats, of which 662 were lost to various causes. U-boats sank nearly 3,000 Allied and neutral ships. In all those sunken ships, and with tens of thousands of survivors, there was only one proven instance of a U-boat firing at survivors in the water. The commander of that submarine, Kapitänleutnant Heinz Wilhelm Eck, was tried and executed for this act following the war. Eck was the only U-boat commander charged with a war crime by the victorious Allies.

The story of Eck's crime begins in the South Atlantic at a few minutes before 8 P.M. on the night of March 13, 1944, when he fired two torpedoes at the 4,700-ton Greek freighter *Peleus*. The ship was sailing in ballast from Freetown to Buenos Aires, Argentina, with a crew of 35 men. The explosion caused the ship to virtually disintegrate, leaving a large amount of debris on the surface, along with half the crew. Eck took two men from the freighter aboard his submarine to ascertain the ship's identity and its destination. With this accomplished he put them back into the water where they climbed into the one surviving lifeboat. Using the excuse that he did not want enemy aircraft or ships to find his location, he ordered his crew to open fire on the wreckage and the men in the water so they would all sink. Several crew members objected, but they obeyed the command, and the U-boat left the scene. They left behind four survivors, three of whom lived long enough to be rescued 49 days later by the neutral Portuguese ship *Alexandre Silva*. The three eventually gave sworn testimony to the British Admiralty concerning the killings. Eck and two of his officers faced a firing squad, and several other crew members served prison sentences.

This type of action—firing on survivors of a ship in the water—was not limited to one side of the conflict. On April 13, 1940, British warships near Narvik, Norway, sank the German destroyer *Erich Giese*. British destroyers then opened fire with machine guns on the roughly 200 men in the water. The Admiralty referred to the incident as an "operational necessity." No one was punished for it.

The history of the U-boat war is replete with instances of a U-boat aiding the survivors of a ship it had just sunk. There are dozens of reports of submarines that had sent ships to the bottom providing survivors with water, food, medical supplies, a compass, directions to the nearest land, and numerous other assistances that helped them survive. In some cases, the U-boat skipper went to even greater lengths to ensure the seamen in the lifeboats left behind had a reasonable chance of surviving at sea. In many instances it is impossible to know what happened to an attack's survivors because many did not survive the ordeal of a lifeboat at sea long enough to be rescued by an Allied or neutral ship.

Several U-boat commanders set the tone for future actions during the first few days of the war. Britain declared war on Germany on September 3, 1939. Two days later the man who would become one of the most famous submariners of all time, 31-year-old former merchant marine officer Kapitänleutnant Gunther Prein, sank the 2,400-ton British cargo ship *Bosnia*. U-47's watch officer first spotted the darkened freighter as she zigzagged just before daybreak. When a warning shot not only failed to stop her but also provoked an SSS distress signal from the *Bosnia*—meaning she was under attack by a U-boat—Prein fired three rounds directly into her. The action silenced the radio and sent the crew scrambling for the lifeboats. However, because the vessel was still moving, one of the lifeboats capsized as it was being lowered and sent its passengers into the water. U-47 crawled along among the survivors as her crew fished them out of the water. Just as all the survivors were put into the remaining lifeboat, a Norwegian tanker came upon the scene. Prein instructed the tanker to pick up the men in the lifeboat, which they did. As the tanker sailed away, U-47 fired one torpedo into the *Bosnia*, which sent her to the bottom in minutes. Years later, Paddy Bryan, one of the *Bosnia's* crew, described Prein as "a smashing feller."

Two days after this, on the afternoon of September 7, 1939, the British steam freighter *Olivegrove,* carrying a cargo of sugar from Cuba to London, was stopped with a warning shot from Kapitänleutnant Hans-Wilhelm von Dresky's U-33. When the British crew was safely off the vessel and into lifeboats, U-33 sank the ship with a torpedo. The freighter's master, James Barnetson, was taken aboard the submarine and his papers examined. Barnetson reported that von Dresky apologized for having to sink his ship and provided him with the proper course to reach land with his lifeboats. A short time later the U-boat returned and fired several distress flares to attract the attention of the nearby American passenger ship *Washington,* which picked up the entire crew and took them to its Southampton destination.

The *Umona* was a 3,767-ton steam merchant ship built in 1910 and owned by a London-based shipping company. On March 7, 1941, she slipped away from the blacked-out docks of London and headed toward Dover, where she joined a convoy south. Her destination was Durban, South Africa. The trip was uneventful, and she unloaded her cargo and a small number of passengers, including five Holy Rosary Missionary Sisters who would play a vital role in the education of black South African children. For her return voyage, *Umona* took on a load of nearly 1,700 tons of peas, beans, maize, and jam, all in short supply in the British Isles. On Sunday afternoon, March 30, *Umona* was sailing unescorted west of Freetown when she was struck by a torpedo fired by a Type IXB U-boat, U-124, under the command of Kapitänleutnant Georg-Wilhelm Schulz. It was reported that Schulz, watching through his periscope before firing the torpedo, could actually see the merchantman's cook in his tall white hat leaning on the freighter's railing, probably smoking a cigarette. Schulz guessed that most of the crew was at lunch.

At the time she was attacked, *Umona* was carrying 107 people. These included the master, Frederick Arthur Baden Peckham, and 84 merchant sailors, 8 Royal Navy gunners to operate the vessel's antiquated defensive weapons, and 14 passengers. The U-boat commander watched as chaos broke out on the stricken ship and at least one lifeboat was lowered. The ship had several fires blazing but did not appear to be sinking. Schulz decided to hold his fire on a second torpedo to send the ship down until the people in the lifeboat were well away. To his amazement, the lifeboat swung around and headed back to the *Umona,* where those in the boat climbed back aboard the ship. Frustrated by this apparently senseless action, Schulz fired a second and ultimately fatal torpedo at the ship. The *Umona* began to sink almost instantly.

The U-boat submerged and left the area as the commander and crew celebrated that they had passed the mark of 100,000 tons sunk, and that Schulz would be awarded a Knight's Cross for this achievement.

Four days later, U-124 was passing through the area where it had sunk the *Umona,* searching for another target, when lookouts reported something in the water. It turned out to be three men on a life raft. They were survivors from the *Umona*. As the submarine pulled alongside, Schulz could see that one man was unconscious and the other two were badly shaken, possibly in shock. After learning their identity, he asked why they had returned to the stricken vessel. One of the men responded that the master ordered them back, saying the ship was not sinking. Puzzled by this because the master should have known that the submarine would fire a second torpedo to send the ship to the bottom, Schulz explained to the men that he could not bring them aboard his boat because it was against his orders and besides, he still had a long cruise ahead of him. He gave them a supply of cognac, water, and cigarettes. Suddenly another ship was reported on the horizon. The German promised to return to give the men directions to land as the submarine quickly pulled away from the raft.

The two conscious survivors of the *Umona* watched in disbelief as the U-boat rushed off, expecting never to see it again. Much to their amazement, it returned a few hours later. Schulz once again apologized for not being able to take them aboard his submarine. He told them they were close enough to shore for the current to get them there in three days, and pointed out the direction of the African coast.

As the U-boat once again pulled away from the raft, one of the officers asked Schulz why he had not told the men that they were actually 200 miles from the coast and had little chance of survival. He responded that he did not want them to give up all hope, even though he thought they had only a small chance of reaching the coast. Fourteen days later the raft with two survivors made the coast. The unconscious man had died on the way, but the remaining two lived to tell of their experience.

On the evening of April 7, 1941, U-124 came upon the 1,746-ton Canadian steamer *Portadoc* sailing with coal and other miscellaneous cargo from New Brunswick. The ship was about 150 miles southwest of Freetown, Sierra Leone. A single torpedo fired from the submarine struck the merchantman astern and she settled down into the water but did not sink. The *Portadoc*'s master, John Evans Jones, and all 19 crew members abandoned ship in two lifeboats. Once the lifeboats were away from the ship, Schulz had 21 rounds fired into her from his 20 mm deck gun, sending her to the bottom. The U-boat crew questioned the survivors concerning the name of their ship, its cargo, and its destination. They then gave the men water and provisions. Six days later the survivors had the further misfortune to land on the coast of the Vichy French–controlled French Guinea, where they were taken prisoner. One man died while held captive, but six months later, the survivors were released in a prisoner exchange.

Early in the afternoon of the day following the sinking of the *Portadoc*, U-124 sank the 2,697-ton British steamer *Tweed*. This vessel was sailing from Liverpool to Sierra Leone, most likely to pick up a load of iron ore from the port of Pepel. The torpedo hit the ship just beneath the bridge and she began to sink almost immediately. The *Tweed*'s master, Henry

Fellingham, quickly gave the abandon ship order, and all but three crew members who had been killed in the explosion managed to get off the ship before she went down. The survivors gathered in two lifeboats. As the submarine approached, the Germans found one of the lifeboats was damaged and had capsized and the men were clinging to it for their lives. Several had been injured by either the explosion or the rush to abandon ship. Schulz ordered the men brought aboard the U-boat, and had his physician, Dr. Hubertus Goder, treat the injured. One of the injured merchant seamen had a dislocated shoulder and a broken leg. After several shots of morphine, the man passed out and Dr. Goder was able to wrench his shoulder back in place and set his leg. He protected it by wrapping it tightly with splints.

While this was taking place, the German sailors managed to repair the lifeboat and set it back in the water with its sails in place. At their commander's instructions, they stocked it with food, water, cigarettes, and even some cognac. Schulz then gave the *Tweed*'s Third Officer Baker instructions for the course that should take them to Freetown. Both lifeboats eventually made it to the safety of the African coast.

Schulz's kindness was repaid in 1958, when he and his wife were invited to attend a reunion of the *Tweed* survivors in Poole, England.

A well-known example of a U-boat coming to the aid of survivors involved the crew of a ship owned by Standard Oil Company of New Jersey, the SS *Esso Houston*. Built in 1938 by the Federal Shipbuilding and Dry Dock Company at Kearny, New Jersey, the 7,700-ton steam turbine tanker was struck by U-162 en route from the oil refineries at Aruba to Montevideo, Uruguay, with nearly 82,000 barrels of fuel oil on May 12, 1942. The oldest active skipper of a U-boat operating in the Atlantic, Kapitänleutnant Jurgen Wattenberg, commanded the Type IXC boat. The 41-year-old Wattenberg had originally been an officer aboard the pocket battleship *Admiral Graf Spree* when she was forced to scuttle herself just outside Montevideo on December 17, 1939, rather than be sunk or captured by an encircling British war fleet. Interned by the Uruguay government, Wattenberg escaped and made his way back to Germany where he joined the U-boat service in May 1940. He had since become a very aggressive U-boat commander, sinking some nine ships over a 19-day period from April 30 to May 18, 1942. *Esso Houston* was one of them. It is possible, as historian Clay Blair has suggested, that Wattenberg's aggressiveness was the result of humiliation over the loss of the world-famous battleship.

Sailing unescorted, the *Esso Houston* followed the instructions to zigzag during daylight hours and on nights when the moon was bright as given by British naval authorities at Aruba when she sailed out on May 9. Just after dark on May 11, 1942, lookouts reported seeing a flashing light once or twice off her port beam. The tanker's master, Captain Trafton Fletcher Wonson, called his four U.S. Naval Armed Guard members to their station, which was a four-inch gun mounted on the deck, and turned the vessel away from the reported light. Fifteen minutes later, when no further reports of the mysterious light were received, the ship returned to her original course.

The following evening at 8:32 P.M. she was about 150 miles east of Barbados when her lookouts suddenly caught sight of a surfaced U-boat crossing their path from starboard to port. The general alarm was sounded and the tanker attempted an emergency turn to starboard, but within seconds the submarine's torpedo hit the tanker amidships on the port side just behind the bridge. Captain Wonson stopped the engines and did a quick evaluation of the damage from this first torpedo as burning oil sprayed over sections of his vessel. He realized the ship's back had been broken and he had no chance of escaping, so after heaving the weighted bag containing the ship's secret documents overboard he sounded the abandon ship alarm. Hearing the signal, Wattenberg waited for the men to get off the ship before firing another torpedo that sent her to the bottom with her valuable cargo.

The 30 crew members, eight officers, and three of the four Naval Armed Guard aboard the tanker took to three lifeboats and a raft. One member of the Armed Guard, Seaman First Class John Oliver Peterson of Texas, died due to injuries he sustained from the first attack.

With all the survivors safely in the lifeboats, the men lost sight of the slowly sinking tanker behind a thick cloud of smoke. Then to everyone's shock and fear the U-boat suddenly appeared from out of the growing darkness and approached them. An officer asked in German-accented English if the ship's master was in one of the lifeboats. Captain Wonson replied that he was and the German asked him to bring the boat closer to the submarine. After following this instruction, Wonson was politely asked the name of his ship, its cargo, the port it had sailed from, and its destination. Satisfied with Wonson's answers, the officer asked if there was a steering compass aboard the lifeboat and if the men required any food, water, or medicine. Captain Wonson replied yes to the compass, indicated the boats were well supplied, and thanked him. To which the German responded, "It's the war, Captain. Pleasant voyage."

The U-162 slowly moved away out of sight in the darkness, but returned about 10 minutes later and informed Wonson that one of his lifeboats, located approximately 60 meters to his rear, was taking on water and in danger of sinking. The captain once again thanked the German as the U-boat slid away for the last time. The seven men on lifeboat No. 3, which was damaged and was swiftly filling with water, were transferred to Wonson's boat. In a later report on the incident, the *Esso Houston*'s Chief Engineer, Charles A. Hicks, claimed, "These (seven) men would have been lost had it not been for the submarine commander."

On May 16, Captain Wonson landed lifeboat No. 1, with 23 men aboard, on a beach on St. Vincent Island. At 1:30 in the afternoon on May 14, the Norwegian tanker *Havprins*, which was sailing east to Africa, picked up the remaining 18 survivors in lifeboat number 4. The following morning the *Havprins* encountered the Latvian steamer SS *Everagra*, which was sailing west toward the United States. After a brief exchange of signals, the survivors of the *Esso Houston* were transferred to the *Everagra*. Three days later, they were safely put ashore on the island of St. Thomas.

Allied propaganda demonizing the Axis powers instilled in many merchant seamen the expectation they would be killed following the sinking of their ships. Several explanations for this fear are discussed by G. Harry Bennett and Roy Bennett in their extensive study of the British merchant navy in the Second World War. One was "Exaggerated dockside rumours, press reports, accusations by leader writers that the enemy often machine-gunned lifeboats, and an alliterative reference by the Prime Minister himself [Winston Churchill] to 'merciless murdering and marauding,' all contributed to their fears."

Most survivors were surprised when they were not machine gunned by the U-boat that had sunk their ship. In some cases, men reported being shot at by the deck guns of a sub after their ship had been torpedoed, but before the abandon ship alarm was given. In reality, more often the vessel had been fired on because one of the following had occurred: the Naval Armed Guard was firing at the U-boat; the ship was continuing to move forward as if it were trying to escape; or there had been no clear indication that the abandon ship order was given. If any of these occurred, the men on board the merchant ship, perhaps scrambling to find a lifeboat, could easily be killed or injured by the firing from the U-boat's guns, but at this point the submarine was probably not even close enough to distinguish individuals, much less target them. In virtually all documented cases, when the stricken vessel had stopped and the abandon ship signal was given, and that signal was either seen or heard by the U-boat, all firing ceased.

Ironically, if the master of a British merchant ship stopped his usually unarmed or lightly armed vessel when told to do so by a U-boat crew member, he was in violation of instructions issued in 1938 by the British Admiralty. These instructions required that a British merchant ship should never surrender "tamely" to an enemy submarine, but should do her "utmost to escape." Most shipmasters knew this was folly. Their chances of surviving a pursuing submarine armed with torpedoes and a powerful deck gun were slim and would likely result in the death of the crew and the loss of the ship.

Such was almost the fate of the American-owned 5,100-ton cargo ship SS *Cardonia*, owned by the Lykes Brothers Steamship Company of New Orleans. With a mixed cargo of 81 tons, the *Cardonia* was unarmed and without a naval escort, sailing from Ponce, Puerto Rico, to Guayabal, Cuba. On the morning of March 7, 1942, her master, Captain Gus W. Darnell, watched as another ship some seven miles off, the American freighter SS *Barbara*, was sunk by a torpedo.

Captain Darnell feared the same fate for his ship and immediately launched efforts to elude the enemy submarine that had sunk the *Barbara*. He increased speed and altered the *Cardonia's* course to bring her closer to the nearest coast. Zigzagging and laying a smoke screen helped him avoid two torpedoes the submarine fired at him, but he was less lucky when the U-boat opened fire with its long-range 105 mm deck gun. The ship took as many as 50 hits from the deck gun before Captain Darnell realized there was no escaping and gave the abandon ship alarm. The signal was evidently heard on board the U-boat, for the firing immediately stopped while the crew abandoned ship. One of the 38 crew members had been killed in the shelling, but the remainder were able to pull away from the burning ship in a lifeboat and three rafts. Once they were clear of their vessel, the firing recommenced until the *Cardonia* began sinking.

The 22 people in the lifeboat landed in Haiti six hours later, while the 15 aboard the rafts were picked up by the USS *Mulberry*. Among the survivors was Third Engineer Robert Edison Dunn, who sometime later told his son about the sinking and expressed his gratitude for the U-boat commander who stopped the shelling long enough for him to get out of the engine room and up onto the deck to make his escape.

The U-boat that sank the *Cardonia* was U-126, under the command of Kapitänleutnant Ernst Bauer, one of Germany's most successful submarine commanders. That month alone he sank or damaged nine ships.

How a U-boat attacked a merchant ship depended on many circumstances, including the weather, how heavily armed the target vessel appeared to be (many merchant ships had more than one gun mounted on it for defense), the visibility of the target, and the predilection of the commander. Sometimes if the radio operator's room was clearly visible it would be targeted first to keep the ship from calling for help and giving its position. This was potentially disastrous for anyone operating the radio when the attack began. Ensuring the silence of the ship's radio was always a priority, as a surfaced U-boat with some of its crew on deck manning the guns and keeping watch was extremely vulnerable to sudden attack. This was especially true if they were within range of Allied air bases. Visibility was usually a problem for the U-boat commander, especially if he were following the instructions given all U-boat skippers to fire their torpedoes whenever possible while on the surface and at night when they were less likely to be seen by lookouts on the target vessel. Most merchant ships ran a straight course on moonless nights, keeping their time- and fuel-consuming zigzagging for daylight and moonlit nights, but they also ran dark, with no lights visible from the sea. If everyone on board the ship followed instructions, including shutting off all lights when a door or porthole was opened, a ship could be nearly invisible to the man looking for it through his periscope or from the rolling bridge of a submarine.

In a few cases, such as that of the 119-ton American sailing schooner *Florence M. Douglas*, the U-boat provided a warning to those on board to abandon ship before she was sunk. The schooner was carrying a cargo of salt bound for Georgetown, British Guiana, when on the afternoon of May 4, 1942, a submarine surfaced nearby flying the German Naval Ensign. The U-boat fired one blank shot then a voice with a German accent hailed them with the instruction, "Leave your boat." The crew did as instructed, and when they were safely away, the U-boat sank her with gunfire. Any possible further contact with the U-boat was lost when the crews of both vessels heard the sound of an approaching aircraft. The submarine quickly submerged and vanished from sight.

Hitler declared war on the United States on December 11, 1941, calling it a "historic struggle." He was correct, it was a historic struggle, but it was also, as Martin Gilbert points out in his history of the war, "perhaps the greatest error" of the entire war. Hitler was not obliged to join Japan's war against the United States—the treaty between them called for such action should one of the signers be attacked. America had not attacked Japan; Japan had attacked America with her bombing of the American installations in the Hawaiian Islands. Although Hitler's motivations remain somewhat clouded, one reason he took this extremely dangerous move was the vain hope that Japan would attack the Soviet Union in return. He hoped this would force Stalin to keep more of his Asian forces in Asia and cease sending them to Europe to fight the German army in Europe. The Japanese failed to reciprocate Hitler's gesture.

Before the declaration was made, Foreign Minister von Ribbentrop is said to have attempted to dissuade him from the move, but Hitler replied that aside from bolstering the alliance with Japan, "The chief reason is that the United States is already shooting against our ships." The Foreign Ministry thought the entire affair a "colossal mistake."

While this declaration caused consternation among some army leaders who perhaps recalled the consequences of America's entry into the Great War, and understood the potential of an America at war in terms of labor and manufacturing capabilities, it cheered the leaders of the Kreigsmarine (German Navy). Grand Admiral Erich Raeder, commander-in-chief of the German Navy, and Vice-Admiral Karl Donitz, director of the U-boat forces, had for some time been urging Hitler to rescind his order restricting U-boat operations in such a way as to prevent provoking action by American warships. Nevertheless, despite this, U-boat commanders regularly reported that United States Navy ships were providing all sorts of aid to British warships, including locating U-boats for them.

In one of the more famous incidents, the USS *Greer*, an old four-stacker destroyer similar to those transferred to the Royal Navy, was heading to Reykjavik, Iceland, from Boston with mail and supplies for the American forces there when she encountered U-562 on September 4, 1941. The U-boat, commanded by a youthful Lieutenant George-Werner Fraatz, was on the surface when it either caught sight of or heard the engines of an approaching aircraft and took emergency dive measures. The airplane was a twin engine Lockheed Hudson British Coastal Command patrol bomber stationed at Iceland. It was an aircraft specifically designed and used for anti-submarine missions. The pilot spotted the sub diving and dropped two depth charges where the U-boat had been. The Hudson's pilot then saw the approaching *Greer* about 10 miles away, flew over her, and signaled that there was a U-boat ahead of the destroyer. The aircraft then returned to the original site and dropped several more depth charges before heading back to Iceland.

The American ship picked up speed, then slowed to 10 knots and swept the area with her radar as she approached the scene. The radar picked up the U-boat and remained locked on her for over three hours. The commander of the destroyer, Lieutenant Commander Laurence H. Frost, never explained why he took such hostile action against the submarine. However, the ship's deck log reveals the story in detail. The British airplane reported the U-boat's presence at 7:55 A.M. Five minutes later general quarters were sounded. Radar contact was made at 8:20. At 9:30, the aircraft swept over the destroyer from its rear and dropped four depth charges where the sub was believed to be hiding and then left the scene, as it was low on fuel. The *Greer* announced it would remain on scene until either contact was lost or a relief plane arrived. At 11:25, a second British patrol bomber arrived at the scene. By now, the U-boat had been attacked by a series of depth charges and was being tracked by a ship's radar. Fraatz must have raised his boat to periscope depth and seen the destroyer. Whether he realized it was an American ship is unknown, but he fired two torpedoes at her. Perhaps because he was submerged and so close, both torpedoes went under the destroyer and did no harm. In retaliation, the *Greer* swept the area with 10 depth charges to no avail. After a second round of nine depth charges, the U-boat managed to break away and the destroyer lost contact with her.

One week later President Franklin Roosevelt gave a nationwide radio address in which he referred to the *Greer* incident as an act of "piracy." His description of the incident makes no mention of the attack on the sub by the British aircraft, nor does it mention that the destroyer planned to remain on the scene until the British could renew the attack or all radar contact with the U-boat was lost. It was all a part of what historian Joseph E. Persico calls Roosevelt's "undeclared naval war in the Atlantic."

Frustrated by his inability to fight back against the Americans, Donitz was fully prepared to take advantage of the new situation. As early as September 19, 1941, he began formulating his plan to launch a series of U-boat attacks along the American Atlantic coast. He called it *Paukenschlag*, which translates into "a roll of drums," later referred to as Operation Drumbeat. On December 17 he summoned six commanders of long-range Type IX U-boats to his headquarters at Kernevel, France, and outlined his plans. The boats would all operate singly, no wolf packs that might be detected by the Americans. They were all to sail to assigned locations off the U.S. coast and on a signal from headquarters begin their attacks as much as possible on the same day. The object was to create a massive surprise attack on the shipping along the American coast. He sent them off with instructions to "beat the waters like a drum."

One boat was delayed, but that month the other five set out for their cross-Atlantic voyage. Among them was U-123, commanded by Kapitän-leutnant Reinhard Hardegen. By the time the operation was concluded, Hardegen accounted for more enemy ships sunk than any of his colleagues. Hardegen was assigned the target-rich area from New York City south to Cape Hatteras. From January 12, the first day of operations, through January 25, Hardegen sank eight ships and damaged one. Having used all his torpedoes, and running low on ammunition for his 105 mm deck gun, U-123 headed for home. Sailing east from Cape Hatteras the following day, this highly successful U-boat skipper encountered the 9,200-ton Norwegian tanker *Pan Norway*. The tanker had left Halifax and was heading to the Lago Refinery on Aruba to pick up a load of aviation fuel to be delivered to the United Kingdom.

The day before, U-123, having no torpedoes left, sank the British freighter *Culebra* using her deck gun. Hardegen planned the same fate for this tanker. In the darkness the sub came as close as she cautiously could and opened fire. Three rounds from the large gun hit the *Pan Norway* and started several fires burning. The shells smashed into the engine room, the funnel, and the large gun mounted on the tanker's rear deck. Three sailors operating the machine guns on the bridge returned fire until the bridge was targeted by the submarine's deck gun, and the *Pan Norway's* guns were put out of action.

Captain Johan Arnt Bach ordered the ship abandoned and had the signalman send the word *surrender* to the U-boat using the signal lamp. Just as abruptly as it began, the firing stopped. The submarine continued circling the burning tanker, but held its fire until the crew had gotten far enough away. Now out of shells for the heavy deck gun, the Germans used their anti-aircraft guns to pepper the hull with holes until the *Pan Norway* sank.

The men in the two lifeboats, one under the command of Captain Bach, the other commanded by Second Mate Oistein Vollebekk, searched the dark waters for other survivors and all feared the U-boat would next turn on them. In retrospect it appears a rather foolish fear since the U-boat had stopped firing its guns to allow the men to get off the tanker. If the Germans wanted to kill them all, they would have kept up the fire until the men and the ship were gone.

In the meantime U-123's lookouts spotted the lights of another ship, so Hardegen turned and raced toward her. The ship turned out to be the Greek freighter *Mount Aetna*, under charter to a Swiss company and therefore flying the flag of neutral Switzerland. She was sailing with a load of wheat from New York to Lisbon. As the U-boat approached, the freighter turned and sped away as fast as possible. It stopped when the submarine used its signal lamp ordering it to do so.

Hardegen told the freighter's master that the survivors of the tanker he had watched sink from a distance were in two lifeboats, and directed him to their location. After picking up 40 survivors, the freighter turned and headed east. Hardegen returned to the scene and came upon another man in the water who had been left behind. He fished the man out, treated his minor injuries, and raced after the freighter, signaling once again for her to stop. When this last man was put aboard the *Mount Aetna*, that ship's captain thanked Hardegen and wished him a safe journey home. The freighter arrived at Lisbon on February 6, with the entire compliment of the *Pan Norway* on board. No lives had been lost because of the attack.

Years later, Second Mate Vollebekk told his son Dan of the incident and explained that the U-boat commander who had sunk their ship was also responsible for saving many lives. Dan told me that his father "was most aware and appreciative of this act of decency on the Germans' part. They could just have easily killed or left them to die in the North Atlantic."

Occasionally a U-boat commander went to extremes to ensure the surviving crew reached safety. One such instance that made headlines involved U-35, a boat built in 1936, and the Greek steam freighter *Diamantis.*

The *Diamantis* was en route from Freetown in Africa to the English port of Barrow-in-Furness with 7,700 tons of manganese ore. At approximately 1:30 on the afternoon of October 3, 1939, while struggling through rough seas about 60 miles from Land's End, she was hailed by the surfaced U-boat and stopped. The U-boat commander, Kapitänleutnant Werner Lott, informed the freighter's master, Panagos Pateras, that he must abandon ship as she was going to be sunk. Captain Pateras ordered the lifeboats lowered, but when Lott saw that the small boats were unlikely to survive for any time in the rough seas, he arranged to take the crew into his submarine.

The arrangement involved one of the submarine's inflatable lifeboats. Since it could hold only four passengers at a time, it required seven round-trips in the dangerous waters to get all 28 crew members aboard the sub. The U-boat crew welcomed aboard the merchant seamen. The rescued men's wet clothes were removed and dried and they were given hot food and cigarettes. Captain Pateras later reported hearing several torpedoes launched, one of which sank his ship.

The *Diamantis* crew remained aboard the submarine until the following day. During that time the Greek master was able to converse with the German commander in English whenever the latter was off duty. At about 5:30 on the evening of October 4, the submarine surfaced some 50 yards off the Irish coast near the town of Dingle, and the men were once again put into the inflatable boat in groups of four. Amid a chorus of good-bye, thank you, and good luck, the Greeks were taken ashore in seven trips.

News of the sub's presence quickly spread around the area and local officials arrived just in time to see the U-boat withdraw. The local people cared for the rescued crew members until they could be transported to England. A report of the landing made headlines in the *Evening News* of London, several Irish newspapers, and was the cover story of the October 16, 1939, issue of *Life* magazine.

Years later, on Lott's 70th birthday, Lord Mountbatten wrote him to express his congratulations for Lott's "magnanimous behaviour" in rescuing the crew of the *Diamantis* and putting them ashore in Ireland.

One of the more unusual incidents involving a U-boat actually rescuing a merchant sailor from an Allied ship concerned an American seaman named Archie Gibbs, two merchant ships sunk by U-boats, and a stay of four days' duration on board a U-boat. When Gibbs returned to the United States following his adventure, he became an instant, albeit brief, celebrity. His picture was taken with First Lady Eleanor Roosevelt, *Life* magazine devoted a full page to his story, the National Maritime Union president gave him a medal, he spoke at production rallies in war plants, and he wrote a popular book. Finally, he was the subject of a heavily propagandized feature film released in 1944. When all the excitement was over and he ran out of money, Archie Gibbs went back to sea.

Archie's tale began after he signed on as an ordinary seaman aboard the Lykes Brothers Steamship Company 8,000-ton freighter SS *Scottsburg* in New York harbor. Also on board was the United States Naval Armed Guard Crew #312, consisting of 10 sailors, including the officer in charge, Lieutenant (jg) Robert "Bob" Berry. Their job was to defend the *Scottsburg* using the single five inch, the four 20 mm, and the two .30 caliber guns that had been mounted on her. Berry had graduated from high school in Sioux Falls, South Dakota, in 1926. He had dreamed of becoming a country doctor, but his family's financial situation made that impossible. Instead, he started at a local Baptist college, working at an uptown department store to help pay his way, and then eventually attended the University of Minnesota and the University of South Dakota as a premedical student. He still could not afford medical school, so he turned to his next love—teaching. He joined the navy the day after Pearl Harbor was attacked.

The *Scottsburg* and all aboard were under the leadership of a genuine old-time sailor, Captain Gustaf Adolph Olofson. The captain had gone to sea as a boy in the days of square-rigged sailing ships. Although he had captained them for several years, he disliked the modern smoke-belching ships, much preferring the old square-riggers instead. This was to be his last voyage. He had taken on the task rather reluctantly, enticed by the large bonus he would earn when the voyage was completed. Like many old salts, he had long dreamed of finding a place on shore to call his own. At the time, he had a small farm in upstate New York on which he had put down a deposit. He planned to use the bonus money to make the final payments and the farm would be his.

The ship—loaded with a mixed cargo that included war material, such as a large supply of TNT—joined a southbound convoy sailing from New

York on May 25, 1942. The *Scottsburg's* destinations were Trinidad, Cape Town, and Basra, Iraq. On the first night out the convoy dropped anchor behind the breakwater on the Delaware River. The second night was spent in the relative safety of the anchorage at Lynnhaven Roads in Chesapeake Bay. It was there that a shipment of tanks and airplanes were lifted aboard the *Scottsburg*. The tanks and planes were lashed down on the deck and covered with tarpaulins. Archie Gibbs was not the only sailor aboard the freighter who felt a U-boat commander looking at the convoy through his periscope would surely be able to see the tanks and planes, making her one of his first targets.

On the 29th, the main convoy broke up and the *Scottsburg* joined 13 other merchant ships and two navy escorts continuing the voyage south. The following day the escorts departed and the merchantmen continued unescorted.

When this much-reduced convoy reached the Serrano Banks, it once again broke up, each ship sailing independently to its first destination. Then, a few minutes after 7 P.M. on Sunday, June 14, the *Scottsburg* was making seven knots 90 miles west of Granada when she was hit by two torpedoes fired by U-502. In the mess room of the freighter, Archie Gibbs and about a dozen other seamen were sitting around, talking, writing letters, and playing cards. The first explosion, which hit the *Scottsburg* amidships on the port side, tossed them all against a nearby bulkhead. The second explosion, about 15 seconds later, increased the chaos and confusion. Archie and a friend, Tex Adams, grabbed their life suits and belts and rushed to the port rail for their assigned lifeboat. When they got there, they found the explosion had destroyed the lifeboat.

Several of the navy men attempted to load the five-inch gun, but it had been knocked loose from its mounting and they were unable to fire it. Lieutenant Berry rushed to the bridge to organize the ship's defense, but found the telephone lines destroyed. For a moment, he watched from his vantage point as his men on the gun deck worked valiantly to fire the five-inch gun. Looking around he realized the ship was quickly sinking, so he ordered the men on the bridge to go to their lifeboat stations. He attempted to blow the abandon ship signal, but the whistle did not work. On the way to his own station, he ran into the captain, who had apparently suffered a head injury and was dazed and a bit confused. He told the captain to get his life vest on and to follow him to the lifeboat, which the captain did. By now they were the last two men on the boat deck, where the water was knee deep. Lieutenant Berry grabbed a line to swing out, but Captain Olofson missed his. Berry swung back over the boat deck, reached out, and grabbed the captain by his life vest. He was surprised when the captain resisted. Berry lost his grip and tumbled into the raft below just as the ship went under. That was the last he saw of the captain.

Meanwhile, after Archie and Tex saw their assigned port-side boat had been smashed, and the port-side raft had somehow been cut loose and was drifting almost a half mile astern, empty, they too headed to the starboard side of the ship. Seeing the lifeboat already in the water, Archie and the others dived into the sea. Fuel oil spilled out of the damaged ship at a rapid rate and soon they were all covered. Archie had the added discomfort of swallowing some of the oil, which made him sick.

The boats and rafts rowed around the area picking up as many survivors as they could find. They attempted to keep themselves as close together as possible during the night. Someone thought it was a good idea to pass around a pack of cigarettes. They decided not to light them for fear the tiny lights would give their position away to the sub, which might hunt them down and machine-gun them all. They waited until morning to light up.

As dawn broke on the 15th, a United States Navy patrol plane sighted them and circled several times. A few hours later, they ran into a lifeboat from another ship. In this lifeboat were the survivors from another of U-502's victims, the *Cold Harbor*, which was attacked during the same night as the *Scottsburg*.

At midmorning on the 16th two blotches of smoke appeared on the horizon in different directions. One was a U.S. Navy warship that circled the area in search of the U-boat; the other was the American steam ship *Kahuku*. The freighter picked up the survivors from both the *Scottsburg* and the *Cold Harbor*. Shortly after, they were joined by another navy vessel that was also hunting the U-boat. Soon the warships gave up the hunt and vanished toward the southwest in response to an SOS signal from yet another ship. The *Kahuku* was left alone. On board were approximately 116 men— crew and survivors. Berry noted that the number of lifeboats and rafts on the *Kahuku* was insufficient for the number of people on board. The ship's master, Captain Eric Herbert Johanson, and her American Naval Gunnery officer, Lieutenant (jg) Kammerer, agreed, but all three recognized there was nothing they could do but hope for the best.

The crew of the freighter did the best they could to help the numerous survivors in their midst. Archie Gibbs and his shipmates were given dry clothes, food, and coffee. Archie was able to wash the oil from his skin, as did the others who had been in the water.

Fearing his ship would suffer the same fate as the two whose survivors he had plucked from the sea, Captain Johanson maintained a high rate of speed and kept to a zigzagging course as he continued on to his destination of Trinidad. Shortly after 9 P.M., a torpedo fired from U-126 hit the *Kahuku* amidships on the starboard side. The captain sounded the abandon ship signal immediately and ordered the lifeboats and rafts lowered. Lieutenant Berry was somewhat surprised, since the vessel appeared to him to be sound and not even listing yet. He went in search of his gun crew from the *Scottsburg* to see if he could mount a defense, but soon found his men had been ordered overboard by the captain.

Unlike the scene following the attack on the *Scottsburg*, chaos now reigned. Berry found himself in a lifeboat under the command of one of the freighter's mates, but the man was unable to get the boat or the men under control. Several of the crew refused to row, leaving it to the Armed Guard members to do the heavy work.

Archie Gibbs had once again jumped from a sinking ship into the oily sea. This time he was not so lucky, for attempts to get himself pulled into a lifeboat failed and he soon found himself adrift among the wreckage. He was going to begin calling for help, but realized that there were so many men calling out, and so much noise from the burning ship, that no one would hear him. It would have been, he later said, like trying to "holler in a boiler room." So he made himself as comfortable as he could, keeping a firm grip on a good-sized piece of wreckage from the freighter so his head remained above water, and he floated in the sea.

Suddenly a large black object loomed up from the sea directly in front of him and threw him into such a fright "it might just have been the Devil." Just as suddenly, Archie found himself being lifted out of the water as if he were on an elevator. When he was completely out of the water, he looked about and realized he was tumbling around on the foredeck of the U-boat.

Before he could react, several of the sub's crew members grabbed Archie and rushed him up the ladder to the bridge, where an officer questioned him as the U-boat fired another torpedo into the *Kahuku,* sealing her fate. The German wanted to know the name of the ship he had just sunk and what cargo it was carrying. He also wanted to know if Archie was a navy man or a merchantman. The officer soon realized Archie was going to be of little help in identifying the other ships his sub had sunk during that last few hours, and asked Archie if he wanted to go back in the water or stay aboard. Archie asked about a lifeboat or a life raft, but was told they had none. The German made the decision for him, saying, "Better you stay aboard." He sent the American below with the men who had grabbed him on the deck.

Lieutenant Berry, who was attempting to restore some order on his life-boat, later reported that while the U-boat was on the surface, a German officer directed men in the water to a nearby life raft in "perfect English." He even pointed his searchlight at several other men who required help. When they had all crawled onto the raft, the sub officer called to them, "So long and good luck." The U-boat then vanished in the darkness. The following day the men in the boats and rafts were all rescued by two United States Navy patrol craft and taken to Trinidad. Archie Gibbs was believed to be among those lost.

Ordinary Seaman Charles M. Dake, recognized for his heroism during both attacks, had, according to the citation accompanying his presidential medal, "single-handedly launched lifeboat number 3, took command and picked up twelve shipmates" when the *Scottsburg* was going under. He also rescued a man from the *Kahuku* after she was attacked. Dake was in the water after failing to launch a damaged lifeboat when he came across the man, who was unable to swim. With great effort, he managed to get the man safely aboard a life raft. For his deeds, the president of the United States awarded Charles Dake the Merchant Marine Distinguished Service Medal.

Archie Gibbs was now a somewhat reluctant guest aboard Ernst Bauer's U-126, whose encounter a few months before with the *Cardonia* was discussed earlier. Bauer gave him a glass of French brandy, and he joined the men who were off duty in toasting what was probably their success in sinking several enemy ships. He did not understand the German they spoke, but he guessed that was what they were doing. Gibbs noted the informality of dress among the officers and men, except for one small thin man who was the only one in full dress uniform. That officer took Gibbs into the wardroom and proceeded to question him. Archie assumed he was the political officer or Gestapo man on board to keep the others in line. He was "heiling Hitler all the time and the others answered him in a tired kind of way, even the skipper."

Archie spent the next four days aboard U-126. Except for the Gestapo man, who seemed to act as if he was questioning a high-ranking enemy officer instead of a merchant seaman off a freighter, the crew was friendly and shared their meals with their prisoner. They talked about their families, and asked many questions about life in America, especially New York City. One man asked him if he knew his friend Benny, who had a store on Manhattan's West Street. One day they were listening to an American radio station when the song "Deep in the Heart of Texas" came on. The crew joined in singing the song in German, "clapping their hands in the right places."

During Archie's stay, the sub fought what he thought was a battle with Allied aircraft, evidently shooting one down but then forced to crash dive as depth charges went off around her. Finally, a few hours from Curacao, the sub stopped a small Venezuelan converted yacht and put their prisoner aboard her. Archie eventually returned to the United States, where everyone who knew him was shocked to see him alive.

Twelve days before sinking Archie Gibbs' first ship, *Scottsburg,* Jurgen von Rosenstiel's U-502 sent an American tanker to the bottom 150 miles northwest of Trinidad. The victim this time was the *M.F. Elliott,* a 6,940-ton steamer owned by the Standard Oil Company of New Jersey (ESSO). At the time she was torpedoed, on the afternoon of June 3, 1942, she was sailing in ballast from Newport News and headed to Caripito, Venezuela. She carried a crew of 38, including her master, Harold I. Cook. Also on board were seven U.S. Naval Armed Guard sailors whose job was to protect the tanker using the four-inch gun, two 50-caliber machine guns, and two 30-caliber anti-aircraft guns.

There is a report that shortly before the *Elliott* was attacked, a United States Navy patrol plane, probably a PBY (Patrol Bomber Consolidated Aircraft Corp.), had spotted a submarine nearby and tried to warn the tanker by dropping flares, but the men on watch at the time did not understand the message.

The torpedo struck the ship on the starboard side aft, and caused a tremendous explosion. Captain Cook realized almost immediately that his vessel "had been mortally struck." He told the radio operator, Edward M. Stetson, to send an SOS message, and ordered all hands to lower the lifeboats. The tanker began sinking rapidly as the men scrambled to get the boats away and get off her. Unfortunately, the ship sank so fast she either destroyed the lifeboats as she went down or sucked them down with her, leaving the survivors clinging to the life rafts that had been launched within minutes of the explosion. The survivors—those who were not killed in the explosion or drawn down with the ship—lashed the four life rafts together and climbed aboard. Captain Cook was among them.

Early the next morning a U.S. Navy destroyer, the USS *Tarbell*, picked up the men on the lashed rafts, and rounded up several others who were clinging to bits of wreckage and a 50-gallon drum nearby. The destroyer recovered 30 members of the crew of 45. The rest were assumed lost, which indeed 13 were. Two others were still alive. They were Able Seaman Raymond Smithson and Ordinary Seaman Cornelius F. O'Connor. Soaked in oil from the ship's cargo, both men clung to bits of wreckage that they managed to lash together to make into a makeshift raft. They had drifted about a half-mile from where the majority of the crew was climbing aboard Captain Cook's large raft, but their calls for help could not be heard.

Despairing of ever finding help, especially as the darkness closed around them, Smithson and O'Connor were shocked to see a submarine passing them, evidently heading toward the main life raft. Two men on the deck of the U-boat heard their shouts, and the vessel turned toward them. Lines were thrown and they were pulled aboard the sub and brought up to the conning tower. They were given some rum to warm their bodies and asked the name of their ship and its destination. O'Connor reports that the U-boat commander spoke perfect English, and when asked, agreed to take them to the raft holding the other survivors. They were slowly heading that way when a flare dropped by a rescue aircraft overhead lit the scene, forcing the U-boat to rush everyone, including the two Americans, down into the boat so it could quickly submerge. For the next three hours, they were guests of the crew of U-502. The German sailors washed the oil from their bodies using a petrol mixture, and gave them graham crackers, warm tea, and cheese and bread to eat. Finally, when it was deemed safe to surface, the U-boat did so. The Americans were brought up on the deck and the commander told them he was giving them the submarine's lifeboat, which was an inflatable rubber dinghy, along with some water, hardtack, and bread. He told them to row six miles south to find their comrades, but in case they did not, to continue in that direction where they would shortly find land. Shaking hands all around and bidding their rescuers farewell, Smithson and O'Connor climbed down into the dinghy. The U-boat commander's final words to them were to wish them well and explain, "This is war, and it is all that I can do."

They followed the German officer's directions, and actually caught sight of several flares and even an aircraft that seemed to be taking off from the surface of the water ahead of them, but they were never able to make contact. On their fifth day afloat, they sighted a tanker and waved their oars in the air to attract attention. The ship, the Brazilian-owned SS *Santa Maria*, pulled alongside and hauled them aboard. Given food by the crew and medical treatment by the ship's doctor, the two quickly recovered from their ordeal. They were landed at Santos, Brazil, on July 1, and along with the other survivors made their way to New York City. Smithson and O'Connor were twice rescued: once by the U-boat that had sent their ship to the bottom, then by the Brazilian tanker.

The following month, on July 30, 1942, U-155, a Type IXC U-boat under the command of Korvettenkapitän Adolf Cornelius Piening, sank its 14th victim since setting out on its first patrol on February 7, 1942. This was only the second American-owned ship sunk by U-155. Piening would enhance his reputation in mid-November of the same year when he sank the British escort carrier HMS *Avenger*. However, on this day his target was a 6,096-ton cargo vessel owned by Lykes Brothers Steamship Company of New Orleans. The *Cranford*, under Master James Henry Donlon, was 250 miles south-southeast of Barbados carrying 6,600 tons of chrome ore and other cargo from Cape Town to the United States via Trinidad when the submarine's torpedo struck her on the starboard side between hold #2 and #3. She began sinking rapidly when the abandon ship order was given. Of the 9 officers, 27 crew members, and 11 Naval Armed Guard sailors aboard the *Cranford*, the death toll comprised 2 armed guard members, 3 crew members, and 6 officers, including the master. The U-boat approached the single lifeboat and several life rafts carrying survivors and asked the usual questions concerning the ship's name, cargo, and destination. Seeing that two of the men were seriously injured, Piening ordered them brought aboard the sub and their injuries treated. The U-boat commander then gave the survivors directions to Barbados, two cans of water, and some matches. He also gave them a towline to keep the rafts close to the lifeboat. He was somewhat apologetic that he could not offer them food, explaining that the U-boat was running low itself. The Spanish tanker *Castillo Alemenara* picked up the 36 survivors of the *Cranford* two hours later.

Also in July 1942, thousands of miles away in the Artic Ocean, one of the worst disasters to strike the Allied merchant shipping efforts occurred when the convoy PQ-17, carrying $700 million dollars worth of war material, including tanks, fuel, and ammunition, was attacked by German U-boats and aircraft. The Arctic became a virtual killing field as 24 of 33 ships sailing from Iceland to the Soviet port of Archangel were sunk. Even in the midst of the chaos and fighting—as some merchantmen with Armed Guard crews fought back, shooting down and damaging a number of planes—several U-boat skippers still found time for the humanitarian gesture of aiding survivors in the water.

In one odd incident, U-376 assisted the survivors of a ship sent to the bottom by another U-boat. At about 10:15 A.M. on Sunday morning, July 5, U-88, commanded by Kapitänleutnant Heino Bohmann, sank the 5,177-ton American steamer *Carlton*. The vessel was loaded with tanks, ammunition, food supplies, and TNT destined for the Soviet Army. As the *Carlton* exploded and burned, the U-boat slipped away in search of other prey. Of the 44 crew members aboard the ship at the time, two were killed in the blast. The remainder abandoned ship but found all the lifeboats but one destroyed, so the 42 men crowded into the one lifeboat and onto four life rafts.

At 2 P.M. that afternoon, a German seaplane landed and took two of the men aboard. Over the next few hours, several more German aircraft landed near the group and removed whatever number of men they could safely take on board. Finally 14 crew members and three Armed Guard sailors all crowded into the one 32-foot-long lifeboat were left to their own devices. Still adrift on July 10, the men spotted an aircraft approaching. It turned out to be a British patrol plane. It circled the lifeboat several times then dropped a package into the water nearby, which was quickly recovered. The package contained a rubber life suit, a quantity of corned beef, some hardtack, and biscuits. Generating the most hope among the *Carlton*'s survivors was a note indicating that help was on the way.

Believing in the message, which later proved inaccurate, as desperately as they wanted to, the men who had been on very short rations enjoyed the bounty that had fallen from the sky and awaited the help that never arrived. What did arrive three days later, on Monday, July 13, was a surfaced U-boat coming to investigate the small spot on the horizon reported by one of its lookouts. U-376, commanded by Kapitänleutnant Friedrich-Karl Marks, had luckily for the *Carlton* survivors sunk an abandoned American cargo vessel three days earlier. Before sinking the *Hoosier*, whose crew had been taken away by a British corvette, the Germans searched her and recovered a quantity of blankets and other supplies. Marks asked the men in the *Carlton*'s lifeboat what ship they were from and if they needed any medical assistance. They responded in the negative to the last question. Marks then told them he was sorry he could not take them aboard his submarine. He explained he was just outbound on patrol, but he did give them 10 packages of blankets his men had taken from the *Hoosier*, as well as a 10-gallon container of fresh water, some foodstuffs, a compass, cigarettes, and the course to either Russia or Germany. They could decide themselves where to go. Marks told the men he was sorry for their predicament, and wished them good luck as his submarine departed.

The *Carlton*'s first assistant engineer died soon after, and was buried at sea as best as the small boat could handle. A few days later, the American seamen landed near a small village at the very northern tip of Norway. The people of the village fed and looked after them until a German patrol boat came by and took them away. Eventually they were taken to a prison camp in Germany.

While it is true that the history of the U-boat war is full of examples of submarine skippers aiding in some way the survivors of their victims, this in no way implies that all U-boat commanders were so inclined. In many instances, U-boats slipped quickly away, leaving survivors to fend for themselves as best they could. Submarine skippers were under strict admonition from their commander not to endanger their boat while trying to assist survivors. Some followed this to the letter while others did not. It would appear from the records of the boats themselves that U-boats generally made some effort to aid survivors in lifeboats and on rafts if conditions were favorable. For the most part, they were not the crazed Nazis that wartime films made them out to be.

Even the history of the World War I U-boat war, although not as thoroughly documented, has many examples of U-boats aiding the survivors of their targets. In one such case, the HMS *Tara*, a civilian ship requisitioned by the Admiralty and fitted out for patrol duty in the Mediterranean, was attacked and sunk by U-35 on November 15, 1915. Ninety-three members of the crew of 104 managed to survive the torpedo explosion and abandoned the ship in three lifeboats. The U-boat surfaced and took them in tow upon seeing the overcrowded lifeboats, even allowing some of the sailors to seek safety on the deck of the submarine. They were put ashore at a point along the Egyptian coast controlled by Turkish forces, which were allied to Germany. Before departing, the U-boat crew gave the survivors water and biscuits. Unfortunately for the British crew, they were handed over to a Turkish ally called the Senussi. This Islamic sect was greatly influenced by the Wahhabi movement of Arabia, so their treatment declined rapidly until a British Army force rescued them on March 17, 1916.

As in the Second World War, once the United States entered the war in April 1917, German U-boats began operating off the American eastern coast. According to a lengthy contemporary report in the *New York Times*, in a matter of a week one U-boat sank five ships. In each case the ships were stopped with a warning shot and boarded by an officer and men from the submarine. The American crews were given a brief time to gather up their personal belongings and lower their ship's lifeboats. They were then taken aboard the sub, and the lifeboats were lashed to the U-boat's deck. Close to the New Jersey shore all the crews were put back into lifeboats, given bread and supplies of water, and wished a safe journey home. One of the Americans told the *Times*, "The German skipper treated us decently."

In 1915 Captain Alfred M. Snow, a commercial fisherman from Yarmouth, Nova Scotia, was fishing the Georges Bank region from his two-mastered schooner when he and his crew were suddenly surprised by a German submarine that surfaced nearby. Snow later told authorities that the German sailors were very cold and starving. The U-boat skipper, whom Snow described as polite and apologetic, sent his men aboard the fishing boat to gather up all the blankets, clothing, and food they could find. He then told Snow he was going to have to sink his boat once the crew abandoned ship and were safely into the lifeboats.

Perhaps the feelings of most U-boat skippers were best expressed nearly 40 years after the end of the Second World War by Karl-Friedrich Merten, who as commander of U-68 sank over two dozen ships from September 1941 to November 1942. In a letter to the *London Sunday Express*, Merten wrote, "Survivors were not considered 'enemies' but as tragic human beings with an extremely uncertain fate. To assist them within the framework of orders and security of one's own ship was a seaman's obligation and duty."

One of those two dozen ships that fell victim to Merten's U-68 was the 2,345-ton motor tanker MS *Arriaga*. Although she was of Panamanian registry, the Petroleum Heat and Power Company of Baltimore owned her, she flew the United States flag, and she was crewed by American merchant mariners. At midday on June 23, 1942, the tanker was traveling about 50 miles off the coast of Columbia, transporting 3,100 tons of fresh water from Baltimore to the oil refinery on Aruba, when a torpedo fired from U-68 struck her. The weapon slammed into the port side, ripped a huge hole in the hull, blew out the engine room bulkhead, destroyed the steering gear and the port lifeboat, and killed Chief Engineer Harry L. Hovland. Captain Gunnar Gjertsen quickly realized his ship was lost. He ordered the engines stopped and sounded the abandon ship alarm. The tanker had a crew of 25, which included two sailors assigned from the Naval Armed Guard. The two rushed to their 6-pound gun mounted on the aft, and when the U-boat began to surface some 100 yards away, they opened fire on her. The shells came close enough to drive the Germans back down as quickly as they could to avoid being hit by gunfire. In a matter of a few seconds the tanker took on such a list that it rendered the gun useless, so the two sailors joined the rest of the crew in the starboard lifeboat. All 24 survivors managed to squeeze into the lifeboat and pull away from the sinking vessel.

The submarine returned to the surface, and seeing that the tanker's gun was no longer manned, she moved in close to the lifeboat. Korvettenkapitän Merten, speaking in very acceptable English, asked the name and destination of the ship. Captain Gjertsen answered the questions. Merten then asked if there were any injured men on the lifeboat, to which Gjertsen replied that one of the gunners had injured his back and his eyes were filled with oil. The German crew members on the deck helped the sailor board the submarine, and he was taken into the conning tower and treated by the boat's doctor. While they waited, Merten had five packs of German cigarettes and 10 boxes of French matches passed down to the lifeboat. He also gave Gjertsen the distance and directions to the nearest shore. When the doctor was finished, the gunner was helped back into the lifeboat. The U-boat skipper wished the men good luck as he departed the scene.

The *Arriaga*'s lifeboat was taken in tow two days later by a Colombian fishing boat and brought to shore. The survivors eventually returned to the U.S. mainland.

Off the west coast of Africa on September 6, 1942, not far from where six days later another U-boat would track a ship whose sinking would live in infamy, the 11,449-ton British cargo ship *Tuscan Sun* was attacked by U-109, a Type IXB boat commanded by Kapitänleutnant Heinrich Bleichrodt. Two torpedoes launched from the U-boat struck the starboard side of the ship close to the engine room. At the time, she was carrying 7,840 tons of frozen meat and 5,000 tons of general cargo bound for Liverpool. Aboard the large single-funneled Blue Star Line ship were 114 people, including 25 passengers and 12 gunners to operate her antiquated defensive weapons. Twenty-two of the passengers, 4 gunners, and 40 crew members, including Captain Edgar Newton Rhodes, managed to get away from the ship in three lifeboats.

U-109 approached the lifeboats and asked if the ship's master was among the survivors. Most likely fearing he would be killed or taken prisoner, they told the German officer the captain had not survived. While learning the ship's identity and destination, Bleichrodt was shocked to see women and small children in the lifeboats. He ordered his men to pass along supplies of milk, bread, and cooked boneless chicken. As this was done, cries for help were heard nearby and the sub's searchlight played on the surface of the water. Clinging to a bit of wreckage was a man in obvious distress. The *Tuscan Sun*'s second radio operator, Gordon Gill, had managed to get off an SSS signal, meaning a U-boat had attacked his ship, just minutes before she began her plunge. He was likely the last person to leave the ship. Now, grasping some wreckage that had been a part of his ship, he was in serious trouble; he had swallowed oil-polluted water and was partially blinded by oil in his eyes.

A line was thrown to him from the submarine, but when it broke, one of the German sailors tied another line around himself, jumped into the sea, and pulled Gill back to the U-boat, where two others hauled him aboard. He was immediately taken below to be treated. The German officer on the deck, possibly Bleichrodt himself, gave the lifeboats instructions for the proper course to reach the nearest coast. As the lifeboats pulled away, someone yelled back to the U-boat, "Thanks, and good luck!"

Gill remained aboard U-109 for 30 days, until the U-boat returned to its base at Lorient. He reported that he was well treated. The oil was washed from his body and some cognac helped him throw up what he had swallowed. He shared a berth with the radio operator and was well fed and clothed by the crew. He told an interviewer that at first he thought Bleichrodt was a "real Nazi," but by the end of his cruise, he knew that opinion was "incorrect."

Germany was of course not the only nation engaging in submarine warfare during the Second World War. Both her major Axis partners, Italy and

Japan, had fleets of underwater craft seeking and destroying enemy ships, as did the Allied nations, especially Britain and the United States.

One big difference between German or Italian subs and the Japanese submarines was the way they treated survivors. Two examples that typify how the Italians responded to the survivors of ships they sank involve the *Marcello*-class submarine *Comandante Cappellini*. Commanded by Captain Salvatore Todaro, the *Cappellini* sank the 5,051-ton armed Belgian steamship *Kabalo* on October 15, 1940, using her deck guns. She had fired three torpedoes at the vessel, but all missed, probably due to rough seas sending them off course. The *Kabalo* had sailed from Liverpool on October 3, 1940, as part of the 25-ship convoy OB.233. Five British warships escorted the convoy. On October 8, the convoy was dispersed so each vessel could head toward its destination.

Captain Todaro decided to take a lifeboat containing 26 men from the *Kabalo* and tow it closer to land to improve their chances of survival. Unfortunately, the lifeboat began to sink, so he brought all 26 aboard his submarine. Three days later the crew of the *Kabalo* was put ashore on the island of Santa Maria in the Azores.

Less than three months later, on January 5, 1941, near the Canary Islands, the *Cappellini* fought a running gun battle with the 5,029-ton British armed steamer *Shakespeare,* during which one member of the submarine's crew was killed. After the cargo ship went down, the Italians pulled 22 men from the water and dropped them off on one of the nearby islands of Cape Verde, then a Portuguese possession.

The Japanese were another story entirely. Tales abound of Japanese crews from both submarines and surface vessels routinely killing survivors in the water or in lifeboats. Most, if not all, are true. There are innumerable incidents in which survivors tell of ill treatment by Japanese sailors. Some recall that Japanese sailors made it difficult for survivors to reach safety, such as when the SS *Henry Knox* was torpedoed by two Japanese subs near the Maldives on July 19, 1943. Loaded with war materiel intended for Allied forces in south Asia, the Liberty ship operated by the Matson Lines broke up after the cargo caused a series of explosions. Captain Eugen M. Olsen succeeded in launching three damaged lifeboats. After confirming all living crew members were off the burning ship, he jumped into the water and was pulled aboard one of the lifeboats.

The two Japanese submarines circled the sinking ship looking for survivors. The men in two boats managed to cover themselves with blankets, giving the impression the boats were empty. The third boat was not as fortunate. The Japanese pulled alongside the boat, removed the sails, charts, food, and water, and pushed it adrift. Two men in that boat died that night.

For 11 days, the three damaged lifeboats searched for help. They finally found a small, uninhabited island on which to land. The following day a passing native vessel picked them up and took them to another island where medical help was available. Perhaps Captain Olsen's log says it best: "Time at sea, 11 days; 28 men survived and 13 men are dead."

By the standard of most Japanese sinkings, the 28 men who survived were extremely lucky. More typical was the fate of the seamen who fell victim to Lieutenant Commander Hajime Nakagawa of the Imperial Japanese Navy. Nakagawa was the commander of the submarine I-37. In one week's time in February 1944, I-37 sank three ships, and each time it machine-gunned the survivors. First was the 7,100-ton tanker *British Chivalry* as it crossed the Indian Ocean. The tanker was struck by two torpedoes on February 22 and quickly began to sink. Fifty-eight members of the crew managed to abandon the burning ship and scramble into lifeboats and onto life rafts. The submarine soon surfaced and its gun crews opened fire on the survivors, murdering 20 men. Four days later the crew of the 5,200-ton cargo ship *Sutlej* faced a similar fate after I-37 sank her. Of the 73 men who made it off the sinking ship, 50 were killed by gunfire from the sub's crew.

Three days later, on February 29, it was the turn of the 7,000-ton British ship *Ascot*. She was heading to Madagascar from Colombo when a lookout saw the track of a torpedo heading toward the ship. The torpedo struck the *Ascot*'s engine room, immediately killing four men working there and bringing the ship to a stop. With the vessel going down, the abandon ship order was given and the men rushed to the port side to lower the lifeboats and life rafts. The starboard side boats had been destroyed in the explosion. Fifty-two men got off the burning vessel alive. A few minutes later, sub I-37 surfaced and opened fire on the ship to hasten her demise. After the sinking vessel finally disappeared beneath the surface, the submarine turned its guns on the crew in the lifeboat and on the life rafts. Tiring of that the sub pulled away, but returned once more to claim additional victims with its guns. Of the 52 men who survived the sinking, the Dutch ship MV *Straat Soenda* rescued three on March 3, 1944. The Japanese gunners had killed the rest.

Although the killings would not be acknowledged by Japan until 1979, Nakagawa had already established himself as a submarine commander with a powerful bloodlust. On the morning of May 14, 1943, while commanding I-177, Nakagawa sent one of his torpedoes into the side of the hospital ship AHS *Centaur*, off the coast of Queensland. This was a clear violation of international law as the ship was clearly identified as a hospital ship and was fully illuminated from bow to stern, including illumination of the large red crosses on her hull. Of the 332 crew, medical staff, and passengers, only 64 survived. The ship was on its way to Port Moresby to pick up wounded soldiers to be returned to Australia. Had the attack happened on the inbound trip, the loss of life would have been even greater.

A terrible fate awaited the crew of the American Liberty ship SS *Jean Nicolet* when a different Japanese submarine attacked her on July 2, 1944. The 7,176-ton cargo vessel was hit with two torpedoes in the early evening as she was carrying military supplies from Freemantle, Australia, to Colombo, Ceylon, and then on to Calcutta, India. Her position was about 700 miles south of Ceylon. The torpedoes were fired by the I-8, under the command of Captain Tatsunoke Ariizumi. Aboard the Liberty ship at the time were 100 people, including merchant crew, Naval Armed Guard members, and passengers.

When Captain David Martin Nilsson gave the abandon ship signal, everyone got off the doomed vessel safely and into lifeboats and life rafts. With the ship still afloat and burning brightly, the submarine approached and a voice instructed the survivors in English to gather around the sub, which they did. Then began an orgy of bloodletting. Some men in the water were machine-gunned; others were brought aboard the submarine, stripped of their personal belongings, and beheaded. Others were forced to run a gauntlet of screaming Japanese sailors swinging swords and pieces of pipe. The killing would have continued until all 100 people from the *Jean Nicolet* were dead, but the sudden sound of an approaching aircraft forced the Japanese sailors back into their boat where they quickly dove for the safety of the sea, leaving dozens of injured on the deck to be sucked into the sea behind it. Many of them had their hands tied behind their backs, making it virtually impossible for them to swim away from the submerging boat.

Reports concerning the number of survivors from the original 100 differ, but the number appears to lie somewhere between 20 and 23. When the submarine suddenly submerged, Captain Nilsson was being questioned inside, along with Gus Tilden, who had triggered the SOS signal that was responsible for the approaching aircraft, and a War Shipping Administration representative named Francis J. O'Gara. Nothing further is known about the fate of Captain Nilsson or Radio Operator Tilden, but O'Gara was later found in Ofuna POW prison camp near Yokohama, Japan.

These examples were neither the first nor the last atrocities committed by I-boat, or long-range attack boat, commanders. Yet neither man was ever forced to suffer the fate of Heinz-Wilhelm Eck of U-852, although their crimes were similar. Hajime Nakagawa, commander of the I-37, was tried as a B-class war criminal and sentenced to eight years hard labor for the machine-gunning of survivors. He was released after six years and died in 1968, 11 years before he was identified as the commander who sank the hospital ship, so he was never tried for that offense.

As for Tatsunoke Ariizumi, the man responsible for the slaughter of most of the *Jean Nicolet* survivors, he managed to escape retribution entirely. His crew reported that he committed suicide as his submarine entered Tokyo Bay after Japan surrendered and they dropped his body overboard. However, great suspicion was raised about this tale, since the submarine came extremely close to shore at one point and Ariizumi could have swam to safety.

Surfacing a U-boat to either identify the torpedoed ship or offer assistance to the survivors was a problematic decision. This was especially true if the ship had not yet gone completely under and was still wallowing, perhaps half sunk and sinking only gradually. Late in the war, the possibility of enemy aircraft suddenly swooping down on a U-boat became an increasing reality, but even during the first half of the war, a partially sunk merchant ship might conceal the instruments of a U-boat's own destruction.

Questioned about his treatment of survivors of merchant ships at the Nuremberg trials, Gunther Hessler, former commander of U-107, described two situations in which he assisted the surviving crew of ships he had torpedoed. The ships concerned were both Greek, the 3,748-ton steamer *Papalemos*, on May 28, 1941, and the 4,981-ton steamer *Pandias*, on July 13, 1941. In response to the question, "How did you help the lifeboats?" Hessler said he told the men in the boats what their position was and what course to follow to reach the nearest land. He went on, "I gave them water, which is of vital importance for survivors in tropical regions. In one case I also furnished medical aid for several wounded men." According to the available records, mostly based on interviews with the survivors, the U-boat's medical officer treated three injured men from the *Papalemos*. In both cases, the survivors were given chocolate, cigarettes, food, water, and rum to help them along the voyage.

Asked if his experience as a U-boat skipper had made him cautious when surfacing around a ship that had not yet sunk, Hessler responded with a firm yes. He then went on to explain what happened after he had fired one torpedo into the 10,305-ton British cargo ship *Calchas* on April 21, 1941, about 550 miles north of the Cape Verde Islands.

The ship had stopped after being hit by the torpedo. The crew had left the ship and was in the lifeboats, and the boat (the *Calchas*) seemed to be sinking. I was wondering whether to surface in order, at least, to give the crew their position and ask if they needed water. A feeling, which I could not explain, kept me from doing so. I raised my periscope to the fullest extent and just as the periscope rose almost entirely out of the water, sailors who had been hiding under the guns and behind rails, jumped up, manned the guns of the vessel—which so far had appeared to be entirely abandoned—and opened fire on my periscope at very close range, compelling me to submerge at full speed.

This incident did not deter Hessler entirely from assisting survivors, as within the next three months he assisted the crews of the two Greek ships he sank.

CHAPTER 3

Undersea Warriors

The submarine tracking the dense smoke on the horizon off the west coast of Africa on September 12, 1942, was a Type IXC U-boat—one of Nazi Germany's deadliest weapons. She was 252 feet long, slightly over 22 feet wide, displaced 1,120 tons when on the surface, and 1,232 tons when submerged. Surfaced, she had a top speed of 18.3 knots, and submerged could make 7.3 knots. This powerful U-boat had a range of 11,000 nautical miles running at a surfaced cruising speed of 10 knots.

A long-range attack U-boat, the Type IXC was armed with six 21-inch torpedo tubes—four in her bow and two in her stern. She normally carried 22 torpedoes stored in various locations quickly accessible to the crew. For fighting while on the surface, she was armed with a powerful long-range 105 mm cannon, for which she carried 110 rounds of ammunition, and two anti-aircraft flak guns, one 37 mm and the other a smaller 20 mm. She had a crew assignment of 48 men.

The Type IXC U-boat's propulsion systems were two supercharged nine-cylinder diesel engines with a capacity of 4,400 horsepower, and two double-acting electric motors for an additional 1,000 horsepower. It was capable of carrying 208 tons of diesel fuel. This fuel supply enabled it to roam everywhere across the Atlantic and into the Indian Ocean. The diesel engines were for use when the U-boat was in transit on the surface, which was expected to be most of the time. The electric motors were for use when submerged, and to power all electrical systems on the boat, including lights and radio. These motors received their power from huge batteries that required recharging on a daily basis. Unlike modern nuclear submarines that can stay submerged for indefinite periods of time, a U-boat was basically a small surface craft that had the ability to run submerged for some time, provided its batteries had been recharged. Charging the batteries required one diesel engine, which in turn required that the boat be on the surface, where it was most vulnerable.

A U-boat making a long voyage, such as crossing the Atlantic to reach the American east coast, would do so mostly on the surface. During the first three years of the war, or at least until the latter part of 1942, this presented only minimal danger. After that, the arrival of long-range bombers and attack aircraft that could fly for hours over the ocean made being on the surface increasingly dangerous. During the last two years of the war, almost all the U-boats sunk by Allied action were due to attacks from the air as opposed to other vessels. According to Gudmundur Helgason, a noted U-boat authority, a total of 264 U-boats were lost due to the actions of ships, 250 were lost to enemy aircraft (both land- and ship-based), and another 37 were lost to aircraft operating in coordination with surface warships during the period from 1939 through 1945.

The Type IXC was the third generation of the Type IX long-range attack boats. Unlike its predecessors, the Type IX boats, which were designed in 1935 and 1936, were oceangoing submarines that could engage in sustained operations far from friendly ports. Larger than the earlier U-boats, they were less maneuverable when submerged and had longer dive times. Despite these drawbacks, the Type IX U-boats, along with the earlier Type VII boats, were the basic strength of Germany's U-boat fleets. Each generation of the Type IX U-boat had some improvements, from the original Type IXA to the Type IXD. These generally involved improved fuel storage capacities resulting in potentially increased range.

Of the 193 Type IX U-boats Germany built, 54 were of the Type IXC model. The Type IXC U-boat tracking the smoke in the South Atlantic on that fateful September day was U-156. Just a year old, U-156 was built at the AG Weser Shipyard in Bremen. Of the 162 commissioned U-boats built by this shipyard, 24 were the basic IXC model. Records indicate the order to build U-156 was issued on September 25, 1939, and her keel was laid on October 10, 1940. U-156 was launched on May 21, 1941, and commissioned on September 4, 1941. Therefore, she was barely one year old when she engaged in an action that would live on in the history of naval warfare.

Kapitänleutnant Werner Hartenstein and most of his crew had been with U-156 from the very beginning. They watched as the boat's construction was completed, including the installation of her engines and her six torpedo tubes. They took her on her trials, which included a dive of nearly 400 feet.

Reportedly adored by his crew, 34-year-old Hartenstein was born in the Saxony town of Plauen on February 27, 1908. He was the only son of a wealthy industrialist. Following two years at a university, during which time he received a pronounced dueling scar on his left cheek, he joined the German navy in April 1928. He then worked his way up from a seaman to a cadet midshipman and then to an officer. Prior to transferring to the submarine force in March 1941, Hartenstein served several years aboard the light cruiser *Karlsruhe*. During the first years of the war he participated in 65 patrols on board torpedo boats, eventually commanding several of the small surface warships. His military decorations included the Spanish Cross (1939), Iron Cross Second Class (1939), Iron Cross First Class (1940), German Cross in Gold (1941), and the U-Boat War Badge (1942). For the events about to unfold in the South Atlantic Ocean, Hartenstein would be awarded the Knight's Cross. Unlike many of his contemporaries, Hartenstein was not married, and had no close ties at home other than the fact his submarine was named for his hometown and carried the Plauen coat of arms on her conning tower. The navy was for all purposes his family and his life.

Hartenstein was about 5 foot 9 inches tall. Historian Jean Hood describes him as "having little of the stereotypical German officer about him." Most surviving photographs show him dressed as a U-boat commander, at sea and smiling. It would appear that the dueling scar running down his left cheek did not detract from a rather "elfish" grin that many reported seeing on his face when he was not engaged in the serious business of war.

On Christmas Eve 1941, Hartenstein and his crew set out into the open waters for their first operational cruise. The U-156's first patrol was to place several weather buoys off the west coast of Ireland. These buoys automatically transmitted vital weather and sea conditions several times a day. This information was of great importance to German naval and air force. On January 10, 1942, she sailed into the great U-boat base at Lorient in occupied France. Her crew was a little disappointed by the fact they had seen no action.

Her second patrol would be much more to the liking of her crew. On this patrol, the U-boat would come within a hair's breadth of influencing the war in a greater way than any other U-boat. She sailed from Lorient in January 1942 as part of a group of five submarines with the mission of cutting off the oil lifeline that ran from Venezuela and Trinidad to North America. Hitler had declared war on the United States the month before, so tankers bringing oil supplies to the United States were fair game for the U-boats.

Code-named Neuland (New Land), the group was composed of all Type IXC U-boats. Three of the boats, U-156, U-67, and U-502, set out first on the 20th and headed for Aruba and Curacao. Five days later U-161 and U-129 left the base and headed for Trinidad. They were bringing the war to the vital Caribbean area. It would take some time, however, as the U-boats used the fuel-saving technique of running only one of their two diesel engines. The crawl across the North Atlantic took slightly over three weeks.

Hartenstein, aboard U-156, was given instructions to attack the Lago oil refinery on Aruba, and also to attack the special lake tankers that transported oil from the Lake Maracaibo oil fields in Venezuela to Aruba for refining. Korvettenkapitän Gunther Muller-Stockheim, who was on his third active patrol in U-67, was instructed to attack the refinery and tankers at Curacao. U-502, commanded by Kapitänleutnant Jurgen von

Rosenstiel, also on his third active patrol, was primarily targeting the oceangoing tankers leaving the refineries and heading north to the United States or east to the war zone in North Africa.

Hartenstein's target was the most important from the standpoint of crippling the Allied war effort. The Lago Refinery was the largest such facility in the world, producing some seven million barrels of refined products each month. The importance of the Lago Refinery to the Allied war effort is clear based on the amount of petroleum products it produced during the war. This included 529,705,800 gallons of aircraft gasoline; 287,553,800 gallons of motor vehicle gasoline; 804,521 gallons of submarine diesel fuel; and 2,949,613,000 gallons of bunker C diesel fuel for ships. The oil was pumped out of the oil-rich fields of Venezuela. Twenty-three tankers owned by the Lago Shipping Company transported it from Lake Maracaibo through a shallow channel into the Gulf of Venezuela and into the Caribbean to Aruba and Curacao. These specially constructed small shallow-draft "lake tankers," as they were known, were the only ships that could get through the channel. Nine had a capacity of 30,000 barrels, and 14 carried 20,000 barrels of oil per trip. After the refining process, large oceangoing tankers transported the product to its destinations. The oil pumped in Trinidad was refined right on the island, and therefore did not have the fragile link between source and refinery of Aruba and Curacao.

Far from being the tropical paradise its location might imply, Aruba is a tiny desert island. It is approximately 19 miles long and 5 miles wide. This makes it only slightly larger than Washington, D.C. Arawak Indians who were fleeing the warlike Carib people, many of whom practiced cannibalism, originally populated it. Most of the people living on the island speak English, Dutch, and Spanish, but many also speak a language called Papiamento, which meshes words from Spanish, Portuguese, Dutch, and English. Aruba is the only place in the world where Papiamento is spoken.

The importance of Aruba, its refineries, and the lake tankers was not lost on the Germans. Donitz wanted his U-boats to make a unified surprise attack on the tankers in and around the island refineries on February 16. His superior, Commander-in-Chief of the Navy Admiral Erich Raeder, disagreed. Raeder wanted the surprise attack launched against the refineries themselves. The Neuland boats left Europe with instructions to attack the refineries before alerting the enemy to their presence by attacking the tankers. Raeder believed more was to be gained by surprising the refinery defenders and causing heavy damage. Donitz was concerned that his fragile boats would be sitting targets for shore batteries as the U-boats fired their deck guns at the refineries. He thought the bigger payoff for Germany and the U-boat crews was to sink the tankers.

The Allies realized the importance of Aruba as well. Aruba was, and remains today, a part of the Kingdom of the Netherlands. When the Germans invaded Belgium and Holland in May 1940, the French military authorities in Martinique sent 180 marines to Aruba to support the rather small Dutch garrison stationed there. On July 6, 1940, two weeks after France surrendered, and nearly two months after the Netherlands had surrendered, the French marines returned to Martinique and were replaced by British soldiers shipped in from Jamaica. Aruba officially became a British protectorate. In early September, the small British contingent was replaced by 520 members of the Queen's Own Cameron Highlanders, fresh from the fall of Dunkirk.

Over the next year, additional forces arrived in Aruba, including a Dutch artillery battery and more Highlanders. The Scotsmen entertained the island residents with their kilt-wearing, bagpipe-blowing parades and concerts. By the summer of 1941, coastal batteries consisting of three 7.5-inch guns and anti-aircraft guns were in place, and the military presence on the small island had grown to nearly 1,000 men.

Based on an agreement between the governments of the United States, Great Britain, and the Netherlands government in exile in London, Aruba and Curacao became American protectorates after the attack on Pearl Harbor. The stationing of United States troops on Aruba was delayed due to diplomatic issues and differences between Rear Admiral J. H. Hoover, Commander Caribbean Coastal Frontier, and Lieutenant General Frank Maxwell, Commander Panama Coastal Frontier, concerning which of their jurisdictions included Aruba and Curacao. Following some confused orders in which both commands prepared to send troops to the two islands, the issue was finally settled under General Maxwell's command. According to official army historians, the primary reason troops were delayed was the resistance of the Dutch government in allowing Venezuela to participate in the defense of the islands. This was probably based on a fear that once troops from Venezuela landed on the islands, which were nearby and important to its oil revenues, it might become difficult to dislodge them.

In any event, six U.S. Army Douglas A-20 Havoc twin-engine light attack bombers were transferred to the airfields on both islands in mid-January 1942. Three arrived at Dakota Field, Aruba, on the 12th. On January 28, Colonel Peter C. Bullard, designated as Commander of All Forces Aruba and Curacao, arrived at Curacao to prepare for the arrival of the American troops.

The defense of Aruba by American forces finally began on February 11, 1942, with the landing of 840 men and officers from Camp Shelby, Mississippi. Known as Force 1280, it consisted of Battery A of the 252nd Coast Artillery; Force HQ and Service Company; Company C of the 166th Infantry; the machine gun platoon of Company D of the 166th; a searchlight platoon; a 37 mm anti-aircraft automatic weapons battery; and a maintenance section of the HQ Battery.

The troops were delivered to Aruba on the SS *Florida*, a passenger liner owned by the Peninsular and Occidental (P&O) Steamship Company of Jacksonville, Florida, that for years had been making regularly scheduled cruises between Miami and Havana. The *Florida* was accompanied by the U.S. Army transport ship *Major General Henry Gibbins,* which brought with it the weapons, ammunition, and other war materiel needed by the troops. The Wickes-class destroyer USS *Barney* escorted them. Two days later the *Florida* departed with the Cameron Highlanders on board, bound for Great Britain, and the *Barney* resumed other duties. The *Gibbins* was docked within the San Nicolas Harbor, which was used by lake tankers bringing crude to the Lago Refinery and ocean tankers hauling refined product away.

Meanwhile, the U-boats of Group Neuland approached their target area at a slow but steady pace. On January 26, U.S. Naval Intelligence reported via radio to the Caribbean Defense Command at Quarry Heights, Panama Canal Zone, that an unspecified but assumed large number of U-boats had entered the Caribbean. The destination of the boats was reportedly unknown, but the report did warn of the possibility of attacks on "tankers from Venezuela" and the refineries.

Aboard the U-156, Hartenstein slipped quietly into the Caribbean on or about February 10, using the Guadeloupe Passage between Guadeloupe and Antigua in the Leeward Island chain. He headed straight for his target—the Lago Refinery on Aruba. Like most submariners, Hartenstein preferred to use his torpedoes to sink enemy vessels and not expose his boat to defensive fire from shore batteries by surfacing and shelling a land installation. He was probably not altogether happy with his assigned task since his boat had not yet sent an enemy vessel to the bottom, and he and his crew were anxious for their first success. Firing shells into an oil refinery or tank farm just did not have the same appeal as launching a torpedo into an enemy ship.

On the evening of February 13, U-156 surfaced off the southeastern tip of Aruba. Hartenstein was able to establish his bearings using the Colorado Point Light, a 33-foot-tall gray square stone tower with a light at its top. The focal plane of this light, which is its height above the water it overlooks, was 167 feet. It was difficult to miss. The U-boat slowly moved along the island's southern coast to the Lago Refinery. The Germans were surprised to see the refinery and the entire area around it completely lit. Cars moved along the road bordering the large tank farm with their headlights on. It was as if the people on Aruba were unaware a war was on and their island was a potential target for attack. Hartenstein made a note of seeing "four large tankers in port and three were at road stead."

U-156 continued its journey along the coast, stopping briefly at the harbor entrance to the capital city of Oranjestad. Once again the Germans noted no effort to black out the city or the harbor. Farther along they came to Aruba's second refinery, the Eagle Refinery owned by Royal Dutch Shell, where they reported yet another tanker tied up to the pier.

As dawn broke, Hartenstein witnessed several American military aircraft that had taken off from an airfield obviously located on the island.

The submarine submerged and moved out into the Caribbean, away from the patrolling aircraft.

What Hartenstein did not know was that the planned American defenses of the Aruba refineries and harbors had not yet been put in place. The heavy weapons of the batteries were still on the dock where they had with great effort been unloaded from the *Gibbins,* along with several thousand tons of explosives. Except for the few Dutch guns that were already in place, the island was virtually defenseless. This information would have been extremely valuable to the Germans.

The U-boat remained submerged the entire day of February 14, and most of the 15th. Hartenstein took his submarine westward and kept far away from his target area so as not to alert the enemy to his presence. His orders, along with those of the other Neuland boat commanders, were to launch the coordinated surprise attack on the 16th. Much psychological and propaganda value was to be gained by having all five U-boats attack their targets on the same day. It would make it look as if there were U-boats everywhere in the Caribbean Sea and surrounding area. Late on the evening of the 15th he surfaced and silently moved in an easterly direction toward the northwestern end of Aruba. At about 10:30, with the island in his view, he turned south and headed directly for the Lago Refinery. U-156 slipped along the surface less than a mile from the shore. When the Germans passed the Eagle Refinery at about 11:30, it was still brightly lit. They could also see a tanker at the pier preparing to load. That tanker was the 6,452-ton American-owned steam tanker *Arkansas,* operated by Texaco. She was to be loaded with refined petroleum products the following morning.

On the evening of the 15th Hartenstein and the other Neuland commanders received a change in their orders with far-reaching consequences. The new instructions came from Donitz and changed the primary targets from the land-based refineries to the tankers in the area. These were more satisfying targets for a submarine captain. Ships first, the U-boat fleet commander told them, then land targets if "the opportunity was favorable."

Most people on the island were going to sleep as U-156 cruised along the coast, unless they had been invited to the Officer's Club at Camp Sabaneta, which had previously been the home of the Highlanders and now served the American forces. There was a reception at the Club for the newly arrived American officers, sort of a welcoming party. General Frank M. Andrews himself had arrived by air to inspect the preparations for the island's defense. He was quartered in a bungalow next to the home of the Lago Refinery's deputy director, which was known as the Guest House. From the front porch of his bungalow, Andrews had an unobstructed view of the San Nicolas Harbor area, including the two lake tankers standing by at the roadstead outside the harbor proper. Those steam tankers, waiting their turn to enter the harbor and unload their cargos of Venezuelan crude, were the *Oranjested* and the *Pedernales.* The 2,396-ton *Oranjested,* which was named for the capital city of Aruba, was the smaller of the two. She was built in 1927 in Belfast. The *Pedernales*, at 4,317 tons, was much newer, having been built in Monfalcone, Italy, in 1938.

The U-boat arrived off the San Nicolas Harbor and submerged just enough to hide from the occasional fishing boat moving around the area and the one Dutch patrol boat they had spotted. Shortly after 1 A.M. on February 16, 1942, U-156 surfaced. The deck crews scrambled to their stations at the two guns or kept watch in all directions. Hartenstein slowly turned his boat so it was directly facing the *Pedernales* and fired a single torpedo. He then turned toward the *Oranjested* and fired a second torpedo.

When the first torpedo struck its target, the *Pedernales*'s master, Herbert McCall, was asleep in his cabin. Awakened by the sudden explosion, he was shocked to see flames sweeping into his quarters. McCall rushed out on to the deck and quickly realized his ship's back had been broken and there was nothing he could do to save her or stem the flaming oil spilling out into the water. He called to abandon ship.

Seconds later, an officer aboard the *Oranjested* burst into his captain's quarters, startling him from his sleep, and reported that the other tanker had burst into a fiery inferno. Concerned over his ship's proximity to the burning tanker, Captain Herbert Morgan told the officer to prepare to weigh anchor and get the ship underway. He wanted to move away from the burning oil as quickly as possible. Morgan quickly dressed and ran out of his cabin. Just as he arrived on the bridge, his own ship lifted slightly out of the water and exploded into flames. U-156's second torpedo had hit its target.

Meanwhile, as the two tankers lit up the night sky and the water around them, Hartenstein turned his boat toward the refinery. On the forward deck, crew members had prepared the ship's 105 mm cannon for action. A shell was loaded into the gun and Hartenstein gave the order to fire once the range of the tank farm was identified. Suddenly the gun exploded and erupted into smoke and flames. Hartenstein and several others rushed down from the bridge to see what had happened. The shell had exploded inside the barrel of the gun and caused the tip to blossom out, making it temporarily useless for further action. Even worse, one sailor, Heinrich Bussinger, lay fatally wounded on the deck. Behind him, the gunnery officer, Second Watch Officer Lieutenant Dietrich von dem Borne, lay badly injured, his right foot and leg badly mangled by the explosion. Furious at the accident, Hartenstein ordered the crew on the 37 mm anti-aircraft gun to fire at the storage tanks. Perhaps if they could set the tanks ablaze some part of that portion of the mission could be rescued. The firing of 16 shells, several with tracers, did virtually no damage to the steel tanks. A frustrated Hartenstein, fearing that nearby shore batteries would soon open fire, ordered the submarine turned about and headed north toward the second refinery.

The explosions and huge oil fires alerted everyone in the area to the attack. General Andrews, who could actually see the burning ships, ordered one of the A20 aircraft to take off as soon as possible. Since there were no lights on the field, and the runway itself was shorter than this type of plane required, taking off and landing was a tricky business. The pilot had to wait until dawn to give him visibility.

U-156 sped along the surface toward the Eagle Refinery as the boat's pharmacist mate worked on the two injured men. When they arrived at the refinery, the Germans found it fully lit just as before. Obviously, word of the attack had not yet reached them. Hurrying to beat the news, Hartenstein fired three torpedoes at the *Arkansas*. The firing was too hurried and sloppy. One torpedo hit its target, but the other two went astray. Hartenstein gave up on any further action, and possibly fearing the arrival of the military aircraft he had seen earlier, dived his boat and headed north, away from Aruba.

The U-boat left chaos it its wake. The *Oranjested* sank where she was anchored. Fifteen of the 25 crew members died because of the attack—most during the flaming holocaust, others within hours. The *Pedernales* did not sink, although her back appeared broken. Of the 26 men aboard her, 18 survived. For hours after, small boats crisscrossed the harbor waters picking up survivors and corpses. The following day tugboats pushed the *Pedernales* up onto the beach for inspection. At Eagle Refinery the *Arkansas* had suffered only minor damage by comparison to the other two tankers. That its tanks were empty and had been degassed had reduced the possibility of a fire. The 37-member crew stayed aboard the ship, which later moved under her own power to a repair facility on the island.

Also killed due to the attack were four Dutch Marines. One of the torpedoes fired at the *Arkansas* had surfaced on the beach nearby. The following day the four men, who were either attempting to disarm the weapon or guarding it awaiting the arrival of a disposal crew, died when it exploded.

It is quite possible that Corporal Bruce Sark of the 166th Infantry, stationed at Camp Sabaneta, Aruba, was the first American in the Western Hemisphere to sound a wartime call to arms on his bugle during the Second World War. His call brought men stumbling from their beds and reaching for their weapons. Unfortunately, the guns capable of actually sinking the attacking U-boat were still on the dock next to the *Gibbins*, not yet assembled. The only weapons that had been set up were the 37 mm anti-aircraft guns of Battery G. The crews staffed their guns, but found themselves virtually blinded by the thick black smoke pouring from the two burning tankers.

According to army records, the smoke from the burning tankers was seen from Curacao, and radar posted there picked up an unidentified vessel leaving the Aruba coast. This was probably U-156. An Army A20 aircraft was sent to investigate. The bomber dropped several flares and even a few bombs, but by then the U-boat had submerged and sped away to the north.

On the night of the 16th, less than 20 hours after the attack on Lago, U-156 surfaced and halted to perform a burial at sea for seaman Bussinger. As for Leutnant von dem Borne, the pharmacist mate told Hartenstein there was little he could do for the officer. The man's only chance of survival was to be taken to a medical facility. Hartenstein contacted the U-boat headquarters in France and, after explaining that the officer's life depended on quick and professional medical treatment, obtained their reluctant permission to put him ashore at the Vichy French base on Martinique.

Traveling toward Martinique, the U-boat came upon the 5,127-ton Hog Island–class steam merchant ship *Delplata* some 60 miles west of the French island. The ship, owned by the Mississippi Shipping Company of New Orleans, was carrying 6,100 tons of general cargo from Rio to St. Thomas.

Hartenstein fired one torpedo at the ship early on the morning of February 20. It struck the vessel on starboard aft, causing heavy damage to the wheelhouse, chart room, and the quarters of the master, Roelaf Brouver. It also caused the cord for the ship's whistle to become fouled, and it kept blowing incessantly. The *Delplata* quickly began to list over to starboard and most of the 53 men aboard her took to the lifeboats. However, the master, seven crew members, and seven members of the vessel's Naval Armed Guard remained aboard.

One hour after the first explosion, the ship remained listing but afloat. U-156 fired a second then a third torpedo into her. As they did this, the Germans came under fire from the guns aboard the freighter. The naval gunners managed to fire 12 shots in the general direction of the U-boat before their ship's list grew so bad they and the last remaining crew members abandoned the *Delplata*. The submarine, upon drawing fire from the ship, withdrew and left the area. All 53 men survived the sinking and watched from the lifeboats as their ship settled in the water but stubbornly remained afloat. Thinking they might yet be able to salvage the *Delplata*, several members of the crew volunteered to join Chief Engineer Alexander Korb in boarding her to see what they could accomplish. When they realized there was no hope of saving the ship, they rejoined the others in the lifeboats. The entire crew was rescued the next day by the United States Navy seaplane tender USS *Lapwing*. After determining there was no way to recover the cargo or the ship, the American warship used her guns to finally send the *Delplata* to the bottom.

For his efforts in trying to save the ship, Korb was awarded the Meritorious Service Award on September 9, 1946.

On February 21, U-156 entered the harbor at Fort-de-France, Martinique. Its arrival caused widespread consternation in the city. After some negotiations with the reluctant local Vichy French officials, a launch was sent out to the submarine and von dem Borne was taken to a French Army hospital where the remnants of his badly mangled right foot were amputated. The French had good reason to be nervous about the U-boat's presence, and sent it on its way as soon as the injured man was removed from the submarine. American ships and planes were closely observing the French possession for any sign that the French warships at anchor there might attempt to sail out into the sea and become active participants in the war. The aircraft carrier *Bearn,* along with two heavy cruisers, the *Jeanne de Arc* and the *Emile Bertin,* and several smaller warships, were sitting out the war in Martinique, bottled up under threats from Allied naval forces in the area should they move. The previous December, U.S. Admiral Frederick Horne, representing the Roosevelt Administration, had concluded an agreement with Admiral Georges Robert, the Vichy French High Commissioner of the West Indies, that effectively neutralized the French Caribbean Fleet and saved them from destruction by the Allies.

The arrival of the U-boat at Martinique was observed by American agents and resulted in an international incident. Admiral Darlan's Vichy French government had been warned by the U.S. government not to allow Axis ships and submarines into the ports of French possessions in the Western Hemisphere under threat of military action. Therefore the French officials were not very happy to see the U-boat entering their harbor.

One result of Hartenstein's brief visit to Martinique was that Admiral William Leahy, the U.S. representative to the Vichy French government, was ordered to immediately meet with Admiral Francois Darlan, commander of the French Armed Forces in the Vichy government. At that meeting, he expressed President Roosevelt's outrage over the German submarine's presence in Martinique. Leahy also renewed the American threat to take action against the French possessions "in the interest of security of the Western Hemisphere as it may judge necessary." He also communicated Roosevelt's insistence that the French warships at anchor be "immobilized within 36 hours." This meant removing vital machinery from the ships so they could not get underway. The French did as instructed, disabling their warships.

The surprise attack planned by Donitz against Caribbean targets on February 16, 1942, was partially successful. In addition to the tankers hit by U-156 at Aruba, the other boats of Group Neuland sank two additional lake tankers, the *San Nicholas* and the *Tia Juana,* as well as a Gulf tanker, the *Monagas.* However, the refineries on Aruba and Curacao continued to operate at full capacity, which infuriated Admiral Raeder.

It took the crew of U-156 almost two days of continued effort, but they were finally able to saw off the broken end of the 105 mm gun barrel. Despite its greatly shortened barrel, the gun remained useable until the submarine returned to its base for a replacement.

The gun was not needed for the U-boat's next victim, a 5,685-ton British tanker sailing in ballast from New York to Trinidad to pick up a cargo of refined oil product. The *La Carriere* was about 70 miles southwest of Puerto

Rico when it was struck by a torpedo in the predawn hours. It took two more of U-156's precious weapons to sink her. Even worse for the Germans, two additional torpedoes missed the target entirely. In the end, five torpedoes were expended to sink a single tanker. The 26 survivors from the crew of 41 were picked up by two passing vessels.

Having expended at least 10 torpedoes in as many days, Hartenstein must have decided to husband this valuable resource and use his repaired deck gun against his next two targets. First was the *Macgregor*, a 2,498-ton British cargo ship carrying almost 3,000 tons of coal from England to Tampa, Florida. She was about 25 miles northwest of Puerto Rico on February 27 when U-156 opened fire and sank her. One man died in the attack, but the remaining 30 crew members and gunners were rescued from their lifeboat by a Dominican Coast Guard cutter and taken to Puerto Plata, Dominican Republic.

The next day it was the turn of the American tanker *Oregon*, sailing with 78,000 barrels of naval fuel oil from Aruba to Rhode Island. The tanker was in the channel between Puerto Rico and Hispaniola when the submarine began firing. First hit were the radio shack and the master's quarters, the latter likely resulting in the death of Captain Ingvald C. Nilsen. U-156 then kept up a steady fire at the hull near the waterline, hoping to induce flooding. The boiler exploded, but for some reason the cargo never caught fire. Four hours later the tanker sank, taking six members of the crew with it, including Nilsen. Thirty men survived the attack.

As for Aruba, General Andrews—for whom Andrews Air Force Base in Maryland was later named—saw to it that no more time was lost in placing the heavier gun batteries. The island was put on a blackout schedule, and air and sea patrols were increased. Had U-156 been able to set the tank storage farm or the refinery ablaze with its 105 mm deck gun, or had she arrived a day earlier and targeted the *Gibbins* before its thousands of tons of explosive materiel had been unloaded, the resulting explosions and fires would have been devastating to the oil port and to the Allied fuel supply for the war. Although several U-boats made some passing glances to Aruba and Curacao later in the year, the islands would never again be the easy targets they were in the early morning hours of February 16, 1942. The islands now followed a blackout policy, the harbors were patrolled by small military craft, and the defensive shore batteries pointed out to sea, making another refinery attack unlikely, or at least very costly.

In a real touch of irony, the Nazi government produced a propaganda poster and a postage stamp showing a U-boat shelling the oil refinery on Aruba. In the distance, the refinery is in flames. The poster claimed, "Thousands of tons of oil burned," and "The oil refineries were destroyed."

U-156 returned to Lorient on Tuesday March 17, 1942, to end its second patrol. During the next five and a half weeks the U-boat was given a thorough refitting, including a new barrel to replace the shortened one on its deck gun. During this time, Hartenstein received his U-Bootskriegsabzeichen medal, which was awarded to men who had successfully made two war patrols since October 1939. On February 2, 1942, he was also given the German Cross that had been awarded him during the patrol. The German Cross was an award created by Hitler that ranked higher than the Iron Cross First Class, which Hartenstein received in April 1940, but just below the Knight's Cross.

Hartenstein set out for his third patrol on Wednesday, April 22, 1942. This would be U-156's most successful patrol, in terms of enemy ships sunk or damaged. Twelve merchant ships were sent to the bottom from May 13 thru June 24, and another was seriously damaged. One United States Navy Wickes-class destroyer, the USS *Blakeley*, had 60 feet of her bow blown off by a torpedo from U-156, killing six men and wounding 21 others. The destroyer had picked up the survivors of an American cargo ship sunk by U-156 on May 18, and dropped them off at Trinidad on May 24. The following day she had resumed her anti-submarine patrol off the coast of Martinique when the U-boat struck. The *Blakeley* managed to stay afloat and eventually made her way to Philadelphia, where the bow was replaced. The one merchant ship that was damaged during this patrol proved a harrowing experience for the crew of U-156.

On May 18, 1942, U-156 was running submerged in the Caribbean Sea when she spotted the Eagle Oil Company's 8,042-ton motor tanker *San Eliseo*, en route to Aruba to take on a cargo of refined oil product. It was early evening with plenty of daylight left, so the U-boat commander decided to take his chances with a submerged torpedo attack rather than wait for night. In doing so, he failed to obey Donitz's instructions to wait until dark whenever possible and fire torpedoes on the surface, not while submerged.

The U-boat fired two torpedoes at the target. Hartenstein watched through his periscope as the first struck the ship on the starboard side of the bridge with a violent explosion. He waited anxiously for the second explosion. On the bridge of the tanker, Captain Peter Johnson regained his footing and scanned the sea to the starboard of his vessel. He saw the wake of a torpedo that appeared to be spinning out of control heading toward the *San Eliseo*. He quickly slowed his ship and watched as the wayward torpedo sped harmlessly in front of his bow. Johnson simultaneously ordered his crew to fight the fire caused by the first torpedo, ordered several sea valves opened to keep the now-listing tanker on an even kneel, and directed his gun crew to fire their 4.7-inch shells at the periscope clearly visible in the near distance. He then regained enough control over his ship to begin a serious zigzag pattern.

The gunfire drove the U-boat down and back, hoping to get out of range of the tanker's gun. Raising his periscope back up, Hartenstein fired another torpedo at the zigzagging vessel. This third torpedo slammed into the *San Eliseo's* number 6 starboard tank, causing widespread damage to the ship's side and bottom, but she remained afloat and continued to move, although her speed was now greatly reduced. Frustrated that his victim was not playing her role properly and slowly sinking, Hartenstein sent his fourth torpedo smashing into her number 3 starboard storage tank. Again, the violent explosion caused a vast amount of damage.

By all reasonable judgments, the tanker should have been doomed and headed to the bottom of the sea, but her captain proved to be as stubborn and determined as the submarine commander, and he fought on against all odds. While the deck gun continued its relentless firing at the periscope, the tanker's main engines suddenly came to a stop. She sat there on the water, awaiting her fate for several long minutes, while her third engineer, G. Brodie, and seventh engineer, Eric Booth, fought to restart the engines.

The engines restarted not a moment too soon, for a fifth torpedo was heading straight for the ship's bow. Captain Johnson used the limited amount of speed he could get from his wounded ship, which was barely five knots, to turn her away from the speeding missile. The torpedo missed the bow by inches.

With growing frustration, Hartenstein decided five torpedoes were enough for one tanker. Instead, he ordered the sub to the surface and directed his gun crews to prepare for battle. As they surfaced the German sailors rushed up to the deck to operate their guns, but to their shock, the tanker was bearing down on them on a collision course. Captain Johnson realized the U-boat was surfacing and that his ship was virtually defenseless against the modern weapons on the sub's deck. Therefore, instead of a one-sided gunfight, he would use his large heavy tanker as the ultimate weapon against the much smaller and more fragile submarine. He would cut her in two.

That did it for Hartenstein. He ordered his men back below and gave the emergency dive order. The U-boat slipped below the waves before the tanker could strike her, and she sped away to the safety of the open ocean.

Captain Johnson used a recent invention that pumped compressed air into the ship's storage tanks to keep her from listing over and to stay afloat. By locking down the tank lids and pumping the compressed air into the tanks, buoyancy was added to the vessel and seawater was driven out. Two days later the badly damaged tanker arrived at Barbados.

For their actions in staying in the severely damaged and burning engine room and restarting the engines, Brodie and Booth were both awarded the Lloyd's War Medal for Bravery at Sea, and received the MBE (Member of the British Empire). Captain Johnson was also awarded the Lloyd's War Medal for Bravery at Sea, as well as the Officer of the British Empire (OBE) for his truly courageous and successful fight.

U-156 began its fourth and most fateful patrol on August 20, 1942. During the summer months, Dontiz's U-boat force had extracted a heavy toll on enemy shipping, pushing the total sunk in the Atlantic to over 3,000,000 tons. By mid-September there were three U-Boat groups operating in the region. Combined with those sailing singly, there were some 17 attack U-boats patrolling the mid- and South Atlantic or sailing through it to round the Cape of Good Hope at the tip of Africa to hunt Allied ships in the Indian Ocean. Supporting the attack boats and therefore permitting them to remain on patrol for extended periods were three U-boat tankers, known as Milch Cows, and two Dutch submarines the Germans had captured and turned into torpedo supply vessels. Finally, four Italian submarines were also patrolling the South Atlantic independent of their German allies. One of these was the *Comandante Cappellini* from a previous chapter.

The *Cappellini* was a *Marcello*-class submarine launched in May 1939. The *Marcello*-class, of which 11 were built, is considered by many to be the best submarine Italy produced during the war. They were structurally sound, fast, and had great maneuverability. At 239-½ feet, the *Cappellini* was 12-½ feet shorter than U-156 and slightly less than 2 feet wider. She had a top speed of 17.4 knots on the surface, and 8 knots submerged. Her crew of 58 was 10 more that the U-boat, which made for more crowded conditions. She was armed with eight torpedo tubes, four near her bow and four at her stern. The Italian's deck armament was more plentiful than on a typical German submarine. She had two 100 mm, 47-caliber deck guns, and four 13.2 mm anti-aircraft machine guns mounted in pairs. She normally sailed with 16 torpedoes aboard, as well as 300 shells for the deck guns and 3,000 rounds for the A.A. guns. Her power plant for surface cruising was two 1,500-horsepower diesel engines manufactured by Fiat, while submerged she relied on two 560-horsepower electric motors made by CRDA. Carrying substantially less fuel that the Type IXC U-boats, the *Marcellos* had less range and thus shorter combat cruises.

Now operating under its third captain, Capitano di Corvetta (Lieutenant Commander) Marco Revedin, the *Cappellini* had sunk five Allied ships—four cargo steamers and one tanker—for a total of 31,648 tons. She had sailed from the submarine base at Bordeaux (called Betasom by the Italians) on August 21, 1942, with instructions to cruise in the mid-Atlantic between Africa and South America and watch for enemy ships leaving either South African ports or the River Plate in Brazil and heading north toward Britain. She was to operate alone, or if the situation warranted, could call on the assistance of three other Italian submarines in the general area.

The Milch Cows were a great innovation for the U-boat fleets. Formerly, the submarines had to either return to their ports to refuel, subjecting them to attack by the British Coastal Command aircraft and destroyers, or were forced to rely on surface tankers for fuel and supplies. The surface tankers were a favorite target of the Allies, and a U-boat was never so vulnerable to attack as when it was connected to a tanker sitting on the surface. During the first few years of the war, British warship captains were known to trail a German tanker from a long distance, hoping to sink both the tanker and a U-boat in need of fuel at the same time. Tanker losses to Allied attacks grew so severe that their use was discontinued in the fall of 1942 in favor of the Milch Cows.

Known technically as Type XIV U-Boats, these undersea tankers were 1,668 tons, and carried 720 tons of diesel fuel. They had an operational range of 12,300 miles. In addition to fuel, they provided the attack boats with food, torpedoes, ammunition for their deck guns, drinking water, and medical supplies. They also carried replacement crew members for the sick and wounded removed from the attack boats. They were not equipped with torpedo tubes, and had no heavy deck guns. Their only defense was several anti-aircraft guns to fight off Allied attack planes. Their normal crew compliment was between 53 and 60 men, depending on the number of spare sailors they carried.

On this patrol, U-156 joined seven other long-range attack boats to comprise Group Eisbar (Polar Bear). The Milch Cow U-459, the first built for this purpose, and commanded by Korvettenkapitän Georg von Wilamowitz-Mollendorf, supported the group. On September 4, sailing on the surface at the far western edge of the group, U-459 spotted what appeared to be a small sail in the distance. Suspecting it might be a lifeboat, Wilamowitz-Mollendorf turned his U-boat toward it. It turned out to be a lifeboat with 19 men on board.

U-459 had come across one of two lifeboats from the 5,441-ton American freighter *California*. The Italian submarine *Reginaldo Giuliani* had sunk the cargo ship on August 13, 1942, not far from Trinidad. She had been carrying 4,000 tons of manganese from Bombay to New York with stops at Cape Town and Trinidad. Reports of the sinking indicate that the Italian submarine fired a torpedo into her, and then waited for the crew of 38 men to abandon ship, whereupon the ship was finished off with gunfire.

The crew abandoned their ship in two lifeboats, each containing 19 men. The boats became separated and this one had been driven out into the ocean by the prevailing currents. They evidently appeared in good health despite their ordeal when the U-boat found them, but were running low on food and were lost. The Germans distributed cigarettes, brown bread, and other food items, as well as water and rum, to the men, who were glad for the extra supplies. When asked if the submarine could take them in tow, Wilamowitz-Mollendorf refused, as it would have required him to remain on the surface and extremely vulnerable to sudden attack. The sailor operating the helm of the lifeboat seemed capable, but he had no idea where they were, so he was shown a chart of the region. Their position was pointed out as were the nearby Cape Verde Islands, and he was shown the proper course to take to make land on the islands. Before departing, one of the German sailors checked the compass being used by the lifeboat to ensure that it was working properly.

This lifeboat, with all 19 men, was recovered the following day by a passing British ship, the *City of Capetown*. The second lifeboat was not found until September 14, when the Norwegian *Talisman* rescued 18 of the original 19 men. One man, believed to be the chief engineer of the *California*, had died from exposure.

The Polar Bear Group had instructions to launch a surprise attack in the Cape Town area, a center for Allied shipping in South Africa, and then consider sailing into the Indian Ocean to sink whatever they could find. On August 27, U-156 caught and sank a 5,941-ton freighter that had fallen behind the protective shield offered by the warships of Convoy Sierra Leone 119. The victim was the British-owned *Clan Macwirter*. She was destined for Hull, England, with a cargo of manganese ore, linseed, and pig iron from Bombay. Eleven crew members, including the ship's master, were lost. The Portuguese warship *Pedro Nunes* rescued the remaining 75, including seven Defensively Equipped Merchant Ship (DEMS) gunners. U-156 resumed her southbound journey.

Also sailing in the South Atlantic, although not a part of Eisbar, were the sister U-boats, U-506 and U-507. Both were Type IXC attack boats, and both were on their third active patrols. U-506 was commanded by Kapitän-leutnant Erich Wurdemann. The 28-year-old from Hamburg had been in charge of U-506 since it was commissioned in September 1941. The boat began its first active patrol on March 9, 1942. In those six months, Wurde-mann amassed an impressive record of 15 ships sunk or seriously damaged.

Thirty-five-year-old Korvettenkapitän Harro Schacht had also commanded U-507 since its commissioning on October 8, 1941. This boat began its first active patrol just three days after U-506. Since then, Schacht had sunk 16 ships and seriously damaged one. Schacht had joined the navy in 1926. His service included several years on light cruisers before the war, followed by a staff position until June 1941, when he transferred to the U-boat service. On at least two occasions, Schacht is known to have provided some service to survivors. These were two American ships—the *Norlindo* sailing from Mobile, Alabama, to Havana, Cuba, and the *Torny*, off the west coast of Florida. In the latter sinking, the U-boat helped search the area briefly for survivors. A third sinking involved another American ship in the Caribbean waters, the *Alcoa Puritan*. She was sailing from Trinidad to Mobile with 9,700 tons of bauxite when U-507 fired a torpedo at her just 15 miles off the entrance to the Mississippi River. The *Alcoa Puritan*'s master, Yngvar Krantz, took aggressive evasive action that caused the torpedo to miss. He then sped away. The U-boat pursued him, firing its deck gun. Finally, after more than half an hour, the ship's steering was disabled and the master ordered her abandoned. The entire crew of 54 made it safely into a motorboat and a lifeboat. The U-boat approached them, but perhaps because they were so close to shore and there was the ever-present danger of a patrol plane passing, it turned away. An officer on board the submarine used a megaphone to call to the men. He told them he was sorry he could not help them, and hoped they reached shore. A short time later, a patrol plane saw them and a Coast Guard cutter was sent to their rescue.

On this, his third war patrol, Schacht would become one of the most controversial of the U-boat commanders. Over a four-day period, he sank six Brazilian ships either in or near Brazilian territorial waters, costing hundreds of lives. He capped this off with the sinking of a ship from Sweden, another neutral nation. There appears to be no satisfactory explanation for his actions, especially as he did not confirm the nationalities of these ships before he attacked them. The impact of this on the Allied war effort was enormous. Many in the United States suspected that influential Brazilians were leaning toward the Axis, thus keeping the nation out of the war and officially neutral. Because of the sinkings by U-507, an enraged Brazilian government declared war on the Axis powers. Among its actions, it sent a 25,000-man-strong Brazilian Expeditionary Force to fight under U.S. leadership in the Italian campaign, along with an air squadron. Brazilian warships soon took up stations in the South Atlantic, and most important of all, Brazilian Air Force bases were opened to United States Navy patrol units, making life substantially more dangerous for the U-boats operating between Brazil and Africa.

Sixteen days after sinking the *Clan Macwirter,* the lookouts on U-156 caught their first glimpse of the dark smoke pouring from the funnel of a ship whose fate would secure their submarine an enduring place in the history of the war.

CHAPTER 4

From Luxury Liner to Prison Ship

The ship trailed by U-156 was the luxury passenger ship *Laconia*, originally owned by the Cunard White Star Lines. Swan Hunter and Wigham Richardson, Wallsend-on-Tyne, built her in 1921 for the Cunard Steamship Company. *Laconia*, along with her sister ships *Franconia, Carinthia, Scythia, and Samaria,* were once among the pride of the Cunard fleet. Slightly less than 20,000 tons, 624 feet long, and nearly 75 feet wide, she had one great funnel, two masts, and twin screws that could push her along at a speed of 16 knots. During her long career, *Laconia* carried passengers on numerous transatlantic cruises connecting Liverpool, Hamburg, and New York, among others ports.

In January 1923, *Laconia* found a place in maritime history as the first ship to circumnavigate the globe using the newly invented gyrocompass. The voyage lasted over four months, and she called at 22 ports. A 1928 refit increased her capacity to 347 first-class, 350 second-class, and 1,500 third-class passengers. She boasted a luxurious salon, library, exquisitely decorated dinning rooms, a garden lounge with potted trees, and a smoking room that resembled an old English Inn complete with an inglenook fireplace. She was designed and built for luxurious cruising.

A collision with the American freighter *Pan Royal* on September 24, 1934, in dense fog while sailing off the coast of Cape Cod caused serious damage to both vessels. They had both sailed from Boston the previous day. The *Pan Royal* returned to Boston for repairs while the *Laconia* continued on to her original destination of New York, where she was laid up for repairs. There were no reported injuries from the collision on either ship. According to the *New York Times* report of the incident, the *Pan Royal*'s captain blamed the collision on the *Laconia*, but that ship's skipper said it was unavoidable due to the thick fog. *Laconia* returned to service the following year.

On September 4, 1939, the Admiralty requisitioned *Laconia* and began converting her for wartime use. The Royal Navy had taken similar action during the First World War, but with similar results, unfortunately for those shipping out on these vessels. Thirteen of the Cunard line's 26 oceangoing vessels were lost during the earlier war; the most famous was the *Lusitania*, whose torpedoing made headlines around the world. During that war, Cunard ships transported over 900,000 men and seven million tons of war-related cargo. In addition to troop transports, they served as Armed Merchant Cruisers (AMC), hospital ships, and one was even used as a seaplane carrier. The ship that U-156 was tracking was the second Cunard liner to be given the name *Laconia*. The first had been converted for wartime use and armed with antiquated guns. She had been sent to the bottom of the Atlantic by a U-boat's torpedo in 1917.

During the Second World War, the Admiralty requisitioned 57 civilian ships for wartime use. Some of these were cargo vessels, but many were passenger liners designed for speedy travel. These ships ranged in size from 6,000 to 22,000 tons.

They were given the AMC designation, the words His Majesty's Ship (HMS) attached to the front of their names, a crew usually made up of naval and merchant seamen, some guns (usually quite old), a white Royal Navy ensign to fly, and little else. These ships sat high in the water, unlike warships, and made attractive targets for German surface raiders and U-boats. Because they lacked the armor plating used in the construction of warships, and did not have the damage control systems of Royal Navy ships, many of the men who sailed the AMCs referred to them as Admiralty Made Coffins.

Although they had very limited use, usually for coastal patrols and convoy escorts, the AMCs did for a time plug the gap caused by the absence of enough Royal Navy ships to fight the war. Ten AMCs were sunk by U-boats, and several suffered similar fates at the hands of German warships in lopsided battles. By 1942, most were converted to less aggressive uses, such as transporting troops to war zones.

In January 1940, *Laconia* was outfitted with two six-inch guns of a very old age, six 12-pounders, and a small assortment of anti-aircraft guns. On the 23rd of that month, she set sail for Portland, Maine, and Halifax, Nova Scotia, with a shipment of treasury gold bullion for safekeeping. For the next few months, HMS *Laconia* helped convoy ships to Bermuda, where they would join with larger convoys for the transatlantic crossing. In August, she began escorting convoys from Halifax to Britain. Halifax was a main point of departure for convoys heading to the United Kingdom. Ships would assemble in the large inner harbor known as Breton Bay. About 40 ships sailed from this protected bay every week and formed parallel columns stretching as far as the eye could see. Often there were as many as nine of these columns.

Canadian destroyers usually accompanied these convoys for the first three days of their voyage, but that was the extent of the coverage with genuine warships until they got to within 400 miles of the United Kingdom. Once they reached that position, British destroyers would escort them the rest of the way. During the long cold voyage in between, they were at the mercy of German U-boats and surface raiders, afforded only the protection offered by an AMC. One Canadian sailor who made several trips escorting convoys across the Atlantic aboard the *Laconia* reported how glad he was when he was reassigned to shore duty in August 1941. He said, with the U-boats roaming freely across the entire ocean, "it was no place for a 'sitting duck' AMC."

In September 1941, *Laconia* was struck from the rolls of the AMCs and sent to the Bidston Dock in Birkenhead, just across the Mersey River from Liverpool, for conversion to a troop transport ship. Early the following year she began making voyages to the Middle East to deliver troops to that war zone. The once proud and beautiful passenger liner had now grown weary and worn from the neglect inherent in constant military service since the Admiralty had taken her over. The luxurious gardens and smoking lounges were gone, as were the library and the well-appointed ballroom. Everything left was for function, not beauty. Her distinctive red funnel, white superstructure, and blue hull were now hidden under a layer of battleship gray. If one looked closely, one could still make out the ship's name beneath the thin gray paint on her bows.

On her final voyage as a troop ship, *Laconia* sailed from England on May 28, 1942, in convoy with 16 other ships, including the battleship HMS *Nelson*. On board were 3,000 British troops heading to the fight in North Africa. The voyage was without serious incident. On August 11, 1942, she dropped anchor at Port Tewfik, at the southern end of the Suez Canal, and disembarked the troops, along with their equipment and supplies. It is safe to say almost every soldier was glad to get off the overcrowded vessel and onto dry land.

Because German bombers regularly attacked the port, *Laconia's* crew had no time to relax. The ship was to reload a new cargo of passengers and be underway within 24 hours. That new cargo consisted of between 1,700 and 1,800 Italian prisoners of war. Poor record keeping at the time precludes a definite number of POWs. The Italian prisoners had been captured during the fighting in North Africa, and came from at least six different divisions of the Italian Army. They were to suffer the most on this voyage, and contributed the greatest number of fatalities in the coming disaster. The prisoners were being transported to England in unusual circumstances. They were going to be used to replace farm and factory workers who were now in short supply in the United Kingdom. Their arrival at dockside in a convoy of 50 heavily guarded military trucks just a few hours before departure surprised the crew of the *Laconia*. These were the first enemy prisoners many had ever seen.

These men came aboard *Laconia* in less than ideal physical condition for a long sea voyage. They were the remnants of a badly mauled army, and thus had little in the way of personal belongs such as extra clothing and food. Witnesses observing them at dockside described them as a pitiful lot with nothing more than the tattered clothes on their backs. What items of clothing they had were mostly uniforms designed for the heat of the North African desert, not for the ship's trip into a colder climate. Despite their unknown future, the relief on their faces as they boarded a ship and left behind the camp in which they had been confined surprised many members of the crew.

In addition to the prisoners, civilians boarded the liner. These were mostly women and children who were military or civilian government dependents (including the wife of the governor of Malta), as well as several hundred British army and air force personnel. Some of the latter were suffering from wounds serious enough to earn them a ticket home.

A second surprising arrival was a group of 200 women prisoners. According to the information given the passengers, these women had been arrested for either prostitution or for unnamed activities aiding the enemy.

One of the youngest of the *Laconia* crew members was Albert Goode, who joined the ship's crew in December 1941, when he was just 15 years old. Albert celebrated his 16th birthday in Cape Town on the ship's first visit to that port, and was now headed for his second stopover there. Born in Bristol in 1926, Albert was destined for the life of a seaman. This was obvious to all when at age 10 he became the first boy to join the newly organized Bristol Sea Cadets.

The *Laconia* sailed down the east coast of Africa, her lookouts constantly vigilant for enemy submarines. She made brief stops at Aden, Mombassa, Durban, and finally at Cape Town. At one port, military police officers took the 200 women prisoners off the ship. At each of these stops, passengers were disembarked, including Italian prisoners who required hospital care, and others came aboard. One of those who joined the ill-fated ship at Durban was a South African member of the Royal Navy named Tony Large. Large had been a crew member aboard the heavy cruiser HMS *Cornwall* when Japanese aircraft sank her on Easter Sunday, April 5, 1942, along with HMS *Dorsetshire*. He was now headed for duty at Portsmouth in southern England.

Also at Durban, another small group of Royal Navy sailors boarded the *Laconia* for the trip home. Although they were heading home for new assignments, they could not enjoy the voyage. Instead, they were ordered to augment the 463 officers and crew of the *Laconia* until the ship reached the United Kingdom. Among the Royal Navy men was Jim McLoughlin, whose father had been the first-class steward aboard the *Laconia* before the war. McLoughlin and a handful of his navy mates were crew members aboard the battleship HMS *Valiant* when she was disabled and sent to the shallow bottom of Alexandria harbor along with a second battleship, HMS *Queen Elizabeth*. Protected within the Alexandria harbor by an elaborate underwater security screen, the battleships and a tanker fell victim to Italian underwater assault teams.

On the evening of December 18, 1941, the Italian submarine *Scire*, under the command of Lieutenant Commander Junio Valerio Borghese, had surreptitiously approached the Alexandria anchorage while submerged. Less than a mile from the entrance to the port, the submarine released three of the slow-moving manned torpedoes the Italian frogmen called "pigs." Each torpedo was outfitted for two men to sit astride it as they would a horse; their feet were secured in stirrups. The six men rode their weapons into the anchorage in the wake of a British destroyer just as the underwater gates closed behind the warship. Once inside, each team approached its target and attached a warhead, each containing 661 pounds of explosives and timing devices, to one of the three hulls. The Italians were captured, but the tanker was destroyed and the battleships remained disabled and unable to leave the harbor until 1943. British Prime Minister Winston Churchill called it "an unusual example of courage and ability."

With the battleships unable to sail and requiring only skeleton crews, most of their ship's companies were reassigned. McLoughlin and several others were transferred to shore duty, primarily patrolling a military installation near Port Said. Except for an occasional air raid, the war was still some distance away, and the men were glad for the respite. Then, what looked to be an even better assignment arrived one day when four men, including McLoughlin, were detailed to escort a group of Italian war prisoners to Durban in South Africa aboard a Polish passenger ship.

Following a brief stay in Durban, the men were told to report to a ship for the trip home to England. They were thrilled at the prospect of going home, since they had not been there since setting sail in November 1939. When McLoughlin realized that he was going home aboard the same ship his father had served on as a first-class steward, the luxury liner *Laconia*, he took it as a good omen that things were going to be all right, in spite of the fact she no longer looked the part of a grand lady of the seas.

At the ship's next and final stop, Cape Town, a few more wounded soldiers were brought aboard. These included Trooper Ernest Arthur Barnes, of the highly regarded Seventh Queens Own Hussars (QOH). Originally formed as a cavalry regiment in 1690 and named for Queen Mary, the Seventh QOH had a long and distinguished history. Barnes had joined the Hussars some six years before the outbreak of the war, and served most of the intervening years in Egypt. When war with Italy came in June 1940, the Hussars fought against Italian forces in Egypt's Western Desert. Barnes saw combat as a tank gunner at Fort Capuzzo, and in several engagements against retreating enemy forces after the fall of Tobruk.

The scene in North Africa changed substantially with the arrival of German infantry backed by large numbers of Panzers and Stuka dive-bombers. British and Australian forces were driven back deep onto Egypt, and the highly prized port of Tobruk was surrounded and isolated from Allied forces. Inside the city, the mostly Australian troops were subjected to regularly artillery and aircraft bombardment. During a failed attempt to relieve the city, Barnes was shot in the left leg by a German machine gunner while climbing out of his burning vehicle during a battle with German Panzers at Sid Resegh. Treated at a nearby field first aid station, he was transported back to a hospital in Alexandria.

Barnes rejoined the Hussars just as the regiment was being equipped with new American-made tanks and shipped to Burma in January 1942 to help stop the Japanese sweep through that country toward India. While at a stopover in Colombo, Ceylon, Barnes, whose leg had never quite healed, was put aboard a flight to New Delhi to have surgeons at a military hospital there examine the leg. The surgeons found extensive bone damage and determined that the leg needed a level of surgical care available only in Britain, so he was put aboard a troop ship heading for home. At Cape Town, he and a group of other wounded soldiers were transferred to a second ship, the *Laconia*. Ironically, the ship he was originally aboard made it safely through the U-boat hunting grounds in the South and North Atlantic to home. The *Laconia* was to have a different fate.

Laconia set out from Cape Town carrying over 2,700 souls on September 1, 1942, and headed into the South Atlantic. In addition to the prisoners and the crew, she now transported about 87 civilians, 286 British military personnel, and 103 Polish officer cadets. The Poles were assigned to guard the Italian POWs who, for the most part, were locked deep in the holds of the ship.

The young Polish cadets had been in South Africa at a training facility when they were drafted for the duty aboard *Laconia*. Among the Poles was Jan Derych, who was born in a small town in eastern Poland in 1923.

On September 1, 1939, Nazi Germany launched an unprovoked invasion of Poland. Nine heavily armored German columns pushed into the country from various points, including East Prussia, Silesia, Pomerania, and Slovakia. Outnumbered and outgunned by the invaders, the Polish Army resorted to sending seven brigades of cavalry troops against German tanks. Polish resistance was swept away by the speed and power of the German blitzkrieg. Sixteen days later Soviet forces invaded Poland from the east under the pretext of protecting the Ukrainian and White Russian minorities living inside Poland. The Soviet invasion had been planned between the Soviets and Germany in a Secret Protocol of the Molotov-Ribbentrop Pact a month before Hitler launched his invasion of Poland. With most Polish forces transferred to the nation's western frontier to fight against the Germans, the Soviets met only light resistance to their invasion.

Once most of western Poland was under his control, Hitler concentrated his forces against the capital, Warsaw. For over a week German bombers and massed artillery pounded Warsaw until the once beautiful city was little more than a pile of rubble. The city's defenders surrendered on September 27, having run out of ammunition, food, and water. The following day Hitler and Stalin agreed to a plan that divided Poland almost in half. The Germans took approximately 73,000 square miles in the west that included the mining and manufacturing centers, and the Soviets got about 77,000 square miles that included Poland's oil resources. The Derych family lived in the Soviet-occupied half of Poland. Jan's father, who served in the Polish Army, became a prisoner of war, and Jan and his mother were sent into exile in Siberia.

Many Poles wanted to join the western nations in the war against Germany, but Stalin was adamant in his refusal to allow them to do so. The German invasion of the Soviet Union on June 22, 1941, changed that, and the Soviet leader issued an order permitting 10,000 Poles to travel west to join the Allies. The response was so great that the Soviets were unable to prevent 100,000 Poles from crossing Soviet territory and finding their way into the fight. Jan Derych was among them. At age 16, he traveled 2,000 miles in 26 days to a camp in Uzbekistan. From there he was shipped to the Middle East where he joined other Poles under the command of Lieutenant General Władysław Anders in what was known as "Anders's Army."

While stationed in Tehran, Derych took the examinations for officer cadet and passed. He was driven into Iraq along with 119 other officer cadets who had also passed the exams, where they spent two weeks at an officer training camp run by the British Army. From there they were sent to Gaza. On May 22, they boarded the liner *Mauritania* and sailed down the east coast of Africa for South Africa. The *Mauritania* arrived in Durban two days later. On the 25th the cadets boarded a train bound for Pietermaritzburg, the capital of Natal, where they took up residence in a large British Army tent camp.

At the end of August, they went to Cape Town. Here Jan and the others briefly enjoyed life in a region free of war. He attended a movie and relished the rare luxury of eating fresh-made ice cream. That all ended on September 1, when 103 of the cadets were ordered aboard the former luxury liner *Laconia*. They were to guard a large number of Italian prisoners of war. Derych later commented that the British officials appeared to believe the Poles would not be inclined toward friendly relations with the Italians. In this they were wrong, for as he expressed himself, "Italy had been 'friends' with Poland for centuries." It was not exactly the type of wartime duty they wanted. The Poles wanted to fight the Germans who had invaded and devastated their homeland.

Much has been written about the conditions under which the prisoners were kept aboard this and similar ships. There were reports of mistreatment and harsh treatment by British officers and even some of the Polish guards. The men were jammed into the holds and so crowded that there was little opportunity for exercise or even proper hygiene. Punishment for mild infractions by one or two men was meted out to all. The language barrier made the situation even worse.

We can only imagine the terror experienced by these men. Most were from small towns and farms in Italy, with little or no understanding of oceangoing ships, and were now packed away in the windowless hull of a ship being buffeted by wind and sea. They had little light, virtually no one to complain to about their condition, and were kept locked behind iron gates, unable to see where they were going or even where they had been.

The condition of the Italian prisoners greatly disturbed the ship's third officer, Thomas Buckingham. On his nightly rounds to ensure that blackout regulations were being followed he routinely walked among the prisoners, selecting a few who looked to be in the worst condition. He sent them to the few spare beds in the *Laconia*'s sickbay. Another man sickened by the filth and the short rations that did nothing but barely keep the prisoners alive was Royal Army Ordnance Lieutenant Colonel A. J. Baldwin. Asked by the officer in charge of the British troops to evaluate the condition of the prisoners, and make what improvements he could, Baldwin cancelled the bread and water punishment the men had been on for some forgotten infraction and arranged for them to get a decent meal. This was followed by getting the men to clean up, including washing their bed linens and cleaning out the toilets, which no one had been bothering to do. He also arranged to have showers installed, so the prisoners would no longer have to face the humiliation of being brought up on deck to be washed off with a fire hose. Baldwin made what efforts he could to improve the prisoners' lives, and they apparently appreciated his concern.

By now an experienced warship sailor, Jim McLoughlin was concerned that the ship was not part of an escorted convoy, and that she was belching a large amount of black smoke from her funnel, but he continued to hope for the best. McLoughlin and two others were assigned to back up the DEMS gun crew that operated the old six-inch gun bolted to the *Laconia*'s stern deck.

The sooty black smoke also disturbed Captain Rudolph Sharp, the *Laconia*'s master. At 62, the 5 foot 11 inches tall and rather stout and solemn-looking Sharp had over 30 years of service aboard Cunard ships. A native of Yell, one of the North Isles of Shetland, he had seafaring in his blood; many in his family had served Cunard at sea, including his grandfather and uncle. One of his sons was a serving officer aboard a Royal Navy warship. Most people commented that Captain Sharp looked older than his years, and perhaps there was good reason.

A superstitious sailor might say there was a black cloud over the captain's head. His uncle, Robert Sharp, had been the boatswain aboard the 11,423-ton His Majesty's Hospital Ship (HMHS) *Llandovery Castle* when a torpedo from a German U-boat sank her on June 27, 1918. The ship went down some 116 miles southwest of Fastnet, Ireland. In an example of cruelty and disregard for the rules governing warfare that was used in anti-U-boat propaganda in both wars, the commander of U-86, Oberleutnant zur See (First Lieutenant) Helmut Patzig, attacked the hospital ship even though it had all its special status signals lit, including its Red Cross lights. He then fired his machine guns at the survivors in the water and in several lifeboats. It was purely chance, and the advice of the submarine's second officer to "get away quickly. It will be better for you," that 24 people in one lifeboat lived to tell the story. Captain Sharp's uncle was not among the survivors.

Among the more than 200 lives lost were nearly 100 doctors and nursing sisters of the Canadian Medical Staff. The attack caused such a stir that the submarine's commander and two of his officers were tried for war crimes by a German court after the war and sentenced to prison terms. The two junior officers were convicted, but Patzig himself escaped punishment by fleeing to his hometown of Danzig, which was separated from Germany by the Treaty of Versailles. As a citizen of that autonomous city-state, Patzig was no longer subject to German justice.

During the First World War Captain Sharp had served aboard the *Lusitania*, and was lucky enough to be among the survivors of her sinking. That great ocean liner was sent to the bottom by a U-boat, taking with it 1,198 lives. Throughout his long career he served aboard an array of luxury liners, including the *Olympic, Mauritania, Franconia,* and even the *Queen Mary.* In March 1940, he was appointed master of the *Lancastria,* a 16,243-ton luxury liner. She was requisitioned by the Admiralty to serve as a troop transport the following month. One of her first missions was to transport British troops to Norway to aide in that nation's defense against the German invasion. The campaign was disastrous and the *Lancastria* had to return and pick up the remaining troops now fleeing before the German onslaught. The ship embarked a much different force in Norway, with "the men dirty and depressed, most of them without rifles."

The former liner's next mission was also an evacuation. Following a successful escape from the beaches of Dunkirk completed on June 4, 1940, the area came under total German control. Thousands of British and French troops fled south in hope of finding another way off the continent. Nearly 50 ships rushed to various French ports to pick up survivors and transport them to England. The *Lancastria* slipped out of Plymouth at midnight on June 15, and headed for St. Nazaire, where she anchored at the Carpentier Roads, just before dawn of the 17th.

Two Royal Navy officers came aboard and instructed Captain Sharp to load as many men as possible onto his ship, regardless of the limits set by international law. It was obvious to Sharp and his chief officer, Harry Grattidge, that this was "another capitulation." Sharp and Grattidge were not happy about the order. They knew that if one of the U-boats known to be lurking offshore attacked their ship, there were far too few lifeboats, rafts, or even life vests for the multitude these officers were going to jam into their ship, but they had no option other than to comply.

No one really knows how many Army, RAF, and civilian personnel, including women and children, came aboard the ship as small boats brought them out from shore in massive waves. Crew members assigned to count the people as they came on board had passed 6,000 long before German bombers attacked the ship at a few minutes before 4 P.M. Four bombs hit their target, one going right down her funnel. The liner was quickly set aflame. Sharp immediately ordered the lifeboats away and gave the abandon ship signal, knowing that there were several thousand more people on board his ship than the life-saving equipment could ever accommodate.

It was a living nightmare as chaos spread like the fuel oil pouring from the sinking ship. Soon the overturned vessel disappeared into the sea, as did most of those unfortunate enough to be aboard her. Although there has never been a definitive count of those lost with the *Lancastria*, in part because no one knows how many people boarded her, estimates range from 4,000 to as high as 7,000. Captain Sharp was picked up out of the water several hours later and returned to Plymouth. He now had the unenviable distinction of having lost more people under his command than any naval captain in British history.

It is likely that Captain Sharp looked forward to returning to England with the hope that maintenance on the *Laconia*, so long neglected by the Admiralty, would clean her hull and overhaul her engines so she would cease spewing the enormous black sooty cloud visible from miles away. A good cleaning of her hull to remove the barnacles and other marine life clinging to it would allow the great ship to once again achieve her maximum speed. Right now Captain Sharp could barely get 14 knots out of her.

Also aboard the ill-fated ship was a missionary nursing sister named Doris Hawkins. Sister Hawkins was returning to England after five years of service in Palestine. She was caring for 14-month-old Sally Readman, daughter of a Scots Grays colonel who wanted to get his infant back to the relative safety of Great Britain.

Royal Air Force Sergeant George Stoneman, along with his 34-year-old wife, Ena, and their five-year-old daughter, June, were heading back to their home in Plymouth. They had only recently been reunited in Durban, South Africa. Ena and June had been among the lucky civilians to escape Singapore before its ignominious surrender to the Japanese, thereby barely avoiding the terrible fate suffered by many prisoners at the brutal hands of the emperor's forces. George had been on duty with the RAF in the South Pacific, which was quickly becoming a Japanese-dominated ocean as the enemy forces swept south, pushing Allied forces ahead of them.

George Fish had boarded the *Laconia* at Durban, and was heading home to England and a new assignment. He had been a stoker on the HMS

Enterprise, an Emerald-class light cruiser, since June 13, 1940, six months after signing up with the Royal Navy. The *Enterprise* had participated in Operation Catapult on July 3, 1940, when British Prime Minister Winston Churchill ordered the Royal Navy to attack a French fleet at anchor near the North African port of Oran to eliminate the possibility the powerful warships would fall into Adolf Hitler's hands.

Over the next two years, Fish and the *Enterprise* took part in naval action in the Mediterranean on the famed "Malta Convoys," in the South Atlantic searching for German merchant raiders, and finally in the Indian Ocean, where she barely escaped the port of Singapore as Japanese bombs rained down and the British commanders prepared their surrender.

In April 1942 the *Enterprise* and two destroyers, HMS *Panther* and HMS *Paladin,* were sent by Admiral Sir James Somerville to search for survivors of the two County-class cruisers, *Cornwall* and *Dorsetshire,* which as discussed earlier were sunk by Japanese bombers. The cruiser *Enterprise* rescued the survivors of the *Cornwall,* including South African crew member Tony Large who was to join the *Laconia* passenger roster for the trip to England. The destroyers recovered the survivors of the *Dorsetshire.*

By August 1942, when the *Enterprise* docked at Durban, she had sailed over 140,000 miles and seen action almost everywhere the Royal Navy had a presence. George Fish was among the crew members ordered off the cruiser and sent to a nearby camp for rest and recuperation. On August 29, the day after his 21st birthday, he followed new orders to board the former luxury liner *Laconia* for the trip home and a new assignment. During the stopover at Cape Town he went ashore and bought himself a new watch, a 21st birthday present, because "there was no one else to do so!"

Before *Laconia* sailed from South Africa, the authorities permitted rumors to spread that she was carrying prisoners of war. It was hoped this would help protect the vessel from attack. However, the ship was not clearly identified as a POW ship, with large letters painted on her sides that would be visible to an officer looking at her through a submarine's periscope. From that periscope, she appeared to be what she had been—a troop transport. Had she been clearly marked with the letters *POW,* it is highly unlikely she would have been attacked.

Passport photo of Polish Officer Cadet Jan Derych, a *Laconia* survivor. Courtesy of Barbara C. Derych.

Photo of Jan Derych taken at the Vichy French POW camp in Morocco after rescue. Courtesy of Barbara C. Derych.

A lifeboat full of survivors from an unidentified merchant ship approaching U-107, the submarine that sank their vessel. BArch, Bild 101II-MW-4290-10/Jordan.

The crew of U-107 pulls the lifeboat toward their submarine. BArch, Bild 101II-MW-4287-18/Jordan.

The lifeboat is made fast to U-107. BArch, Bild 101II-MW-4287-20/Jordan.

Shipwrecked survivors from the lifeboat are taken aboard U-107. BArch, Bild 101II-MW-4287-15/Jordan.

An injured lifeboat passenger receives medical attention aboard U-107. BArch, Bild 101II-MW-4287-11/Jordan.

USAAF crews being briefed on Ascension Island for a mission. National Archives.

Water was in such short supply on Ascension Island it could only be used for drinking and washing. National Archives.

A Martin B-26B Marauder on the runway at Wideawake Field, Ascension Island. National Archives.

A variety of American aircraft at Wideawake Field in early 1944. National Archives.

Five survivors from U-156 cling to a life raft dropped from the U.S. Navy aircraft that sank their submarine. National Archives.

Lieutenant (jg) John E. Dryden describes how he approached and sank U-156.
National Archives.

Lieutenant (jg) Dryden puts the finishing touches on a symbol indicating his aircraft had sunk a U-boat (U-156). National Archives.

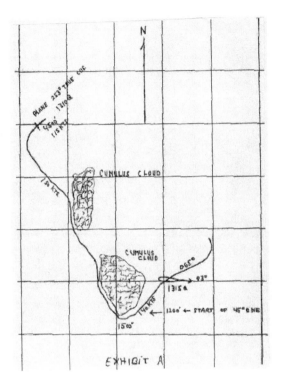

Lieutenant (jg) Dryden's diagram of his approach before attacking and sinking U-156. "Report of Antisubmarine Action by Aircraft," U.S. Navy, USNAS Trinidad, Report no. 7, March 8, 1943.

CHAPTER 5

Wideawake Field

Situated just below the equator in the South Atlantic is Ascension Island. It is almost exactly midway between the bulge of Brazil and the West African coast. The island covers an area of about 34 square miles. It is made mostly of basalt lava flows and cinder cones from ancient volcanic eruptions. The last of these took place approximately 600 years ago. The only green on the island is at its highest point, aptly named Green Mountain. The mountain is located at the very center of the island. As it nears its peak of 2,817 feet, Green Mountain becomes thick with lush vegetation.

Legend has it that the Joao da Nova Castellia first discovered the island in 1501 while he was commander of the third Portuguese expedition to India. Apparently unimpressed by the tiny volcanic island, he never recorded his discovery. Two years later, on Ascension Day in 1503, another Portuguese, Alfonso d'Albuquerque—builder of the Portuguese empire in the east and future viceroy of the State of India—did record his visit, and even gave the island its name.

Still, with little natural growth and hardly any water supply, the island was of no interest to anyone. That all changed in 1815, when the British government exiled Napoleon to St. Helena, some 750 miles to the south. Fearing that French supporters of the deposed emperor might attempt to launch a rescue mission from Ascension, a small Royal Navy garrison was established there.

By the time Napoleon died in 1821, Ascension had developed some genuine usefulness to the British. It was used as a supply station and medical facility for Royal Navy ships engaged in suppressing the West African slave trade. Two years later a small group of Royal Marines replaced the naval garrison. The forces were kept to a small number in part because the island had only a small natural water supply that could be quickly exhausted by too many people. For the next century, the island remained a Royal Navy possession, even receiving the designation HMS *Ascension*. Its classification was as a "stone sloop of war of the smaller class."

In 1922, Ascension Island became a dependency of St. Helena, also a British Overseas Territory. During the pre–World War II years, the island's importance was based on its role as a main relay point for a cable system linking South America with Africa.

With the advent of Lend-Lease in March 1941, the need to deliver as many American-manufactured aircraft as possible to Allied forces fighting the Axis increased dramatically. The U.S. Army Ferrying Command was originally responsible for flying aircraft from their manufacturing facilities on the west coast to the east coast, where many were loaded on ships for the transatlantic voyage, or turned over to a decreasing number of British pilots.

When the war appeared centered in North Africa, American officials looked for ways to get badly needed aircraft to the scene of the fighting. Very few airplanes were capable of flying nonstop across the Atlantic, and those that were could only do so when additional fuel tanks were added and war supplies removed. The shortest route to the war was to fly south to Brazil, and from there across the South Atlantic to North Africa. Although four-engine aircraft could make the trip from Brazil to Africa, most American aircraft were either single or twin engine. Single-engine planes, such as fighters and light bombers, had to cross the ocean by ship. Twin-engine planes could make the hop, but only if they were equipped with extra fuel tanks in addition to other time-consuming and costly modifications—unless they had somewhere to refuel in mid ocean. Ascension Island met the requirement. Having a place to land and refuel in the mid-Atlantic made it possible for twin-engine bombers to cross with a load of bombs and other war materiel, and even for fighters such as the P-38 to fly to the war zone in a matter of hours.

In the fall of 1941, Ferrying Command officials looked at the island as a likely place to build an airfield capable of handling the new and larger bombers then under construction. With nothing to lose and everything to gain, Britain readily agreed to give the United States permission to construct a suitable airfield and supporting facilities. By March 1942, American units were busy preparing to build what became known as Wideawake Field. The military workforce consisted of some 1,300 officers and men, including 77 members of a medical unit. The 38th Engineer Combat Regiment under the command of Colonel Robert Coughlin, along with coast artillery, quartermaster, signal corps, and the medical unit, off-loaded everything they needed from three cargo ships into smaller craft that could approach the harborless island. This included heavy machinery for road building, as well as guns for the island's defense.

One of the officers under Coughlin's command was a battalion commander, Major Frederick J. Clarke, who would in later years become the Army's Chief of Engineers, the actual title of the officer in command of the U.S. Army Corps of Engineers. Construction began on April 13, and by July 10, the new 6,000-foot runway was open for traffic. Supporting facilities, all built from scratch, included camouflaged fuel storage tanks and pumping stations, roads, barracks, a water desalination plant, a hospital, and gun emplacements and ammunition storage depots. Two radar facilities were built, one on each slope of Green Mountain. The 692nd Signal Aircraft Warning Company operated both. They even constructed dummy fuel storage tanks near one beach to serve as decoys for any enemy vessels bombarding the island

This was all accomplished in the middle of an ocean in which German U-boats and Italian submarines roamed at will, yet the Axis powers had no idea what was going on. The secret of Ascension Island remained a secret through the end of the year. Had Donitz realized that an enemy airfield was being built right in the center of his ocean, he would surely have made every attempt to sink the freighters bringing building supplies and construction equipment to the island. By the end of the war, over 25,000 American aircraft used Wideawake Field on their way to North Africa, the Middle East, and Europe. It became one of the most strategically important bases for the Air Transport Command (ATC), which took over the duties of the Ferrying Command in June 1942.

The secrecy around Ascension Island's conversion to an American air base was so tight that it almost resulted in the downing of a British airplane. On June 15, 1942, three days after the runway was completed and ready for use, a Royal Navy Fairy Swordfish torpedo bomber biplane approached the island unannounced. The aircraft had flown off the deck of the escort carrier HMS *Archer* in search of survivors from the *Lyle Park*, which was sunk on the evening of June 11 by the disguised German raider *Michel*. The crew of the Swordfish, Lieutenant E. Dixon Child, Sub Lieutenant P. Shaw, and Petty Officer W. Townson, intended to drop a message to the radio station to signal the Admiralty concerning the sinking. They had no idea an air base had been built on the island. They also did not know that the Americans intended to keep their secret base a secret as long as possible. One method was a standing order to fire at any aircraft approaching unannounced. Lieutenant Child did not attempt to announce his arrival because he was simply dropping a message for radio transmission. Much to the crew's surprise, they drew anti-aircraft fire from the island, with several shells hitting the plane. When someone on the ground realized they were shooting at a British aircraft, they stopped firing. Seeing the airfield before him, Child decided to land and investigate. Three hours later, he took off and returned to his ship. As a result of this incident, the first aircraft to land at Wideawake Field was British, not American.

The first American aircraft to land at the new runway was on July 10, when an army plane brought 10 officers from Accra, capital of the Gold Coast Colony in Africa, to inspect the new facility. The following day they left, flying west to Natal, Brazil. Nine days later, the first 14 U.S. Army aircraft to be stationed on Ascension Island arrived.

Despite the installation of a radio beacon to provide a "Homing-Beam" to assist approaching pilots in locating the airfield, many of the ATC pilots making the trip from Brazil to Africa and beyond were concerned about finding the tiny speck of an island in the vast ocean. A pilot failing to locate the tiny island would be unable to land anywhere before he ran out of fuel. Ditching in the ocean at that time was an invariably fatal incident, as the chances of surviving long enough to be rescued were minuscule. As a result, some talented individual created an aviator's ditty that made the rounds: "If I don't hit Ascension, my wife will get a pension."

The airfield got its name from the sooty tern birds, known locally as "wide awakes" because their screeching sounded as if they were yelling "wide awake." The sooty tern is a large tropical sea bird that can remain at sea, either floating on the surface of the water or soaring above it, for years. It has a wingspan of between 34 and 37 inches. They only come to land to lay their eggs and through the 30-day incubation period. On Ascension Island they habitually returned each year in late spring and early summer to lay their eggs a short distance from the end of what was now an important military runway.

If they remained quietly on their nests, there would have been no problem, but the roar of an aircraft engine speeding down the runway sent them into convulsions of flight as hundreds flew right into the path of the airplanes. Smaller planes could usually fly over them, but the larger heavy aircraft were forced to fly directly into the flocks, killing birds and endangering the planes and their crews. Getting the birds to nest somewhere else became a major objective of the Air Transport Command. Smoke candles were tried, as were dynamite blasts, but to no avail. A planeload of cats was brought in with the hope that the felines would scare the terns away. Instead, the cats were quickly killed and consumed by boobies, an even larger sea bird that otherwise did not interfere with flight operations.

Finally, out of desperation, the Army asked for help from one of the world's leading ornithologists, Dr. James P. Chapin, of the American Museum of Natural History in New York City. Dr. Chapin built a renowned career as an expert on African birds beginning at age 19 when he joined the museum-sponsored expedition of German zoologist Herbert Lang to the Belgian Congo in 1909. His reputation was solidified as a leading authority in African and related birds when he wrote the four-volume *Birds of the Belgian Congo* as a result of the Lang expedition. After secretly visiting the island, Dr. Chapin advised the army that if the eggs in the nests were destroyed before the young were born, the birds would not return to the same nesting ground. It took the smashing of some 40,000 eggs, but in the end, the sooty terns moved to other nesting sites around the island.

On August 19, the forces that had built the runway and other facilities were withdrawn. They were sent to Leopoldville, Belgian Congo, to construct an airport there suitable for military use.

By September 1942, the Army Air Force's First Composite Squadron was operational at Wideawake Field. Under the command of Captain Robert C. Richardson III, the squadron engaged in defense of the island as well as antisubmarine warfare patrols around Ascension Island. To accomplish this task it had 16 Bell P-39 fighters, and five twin-engine Boeing B-25s, known as Mitchell Bombers. Lieutenant Colonel Jimmy Doolittle made the Mitchells famous when he and his men flew 16 of the B-25s off the deck of the USS *Hornet* and bombed Japanese cities in April 1942.

The Army garrison of some 1,700 men was under the overall command of an infantry officer, Colonel Ross O. Baldwin. Reporting to him and in charge of the airfield was Colonel James A. Ronin. Squadron Commander Captain Richardson reported to Colonel Ronin.

Shortly before U-156 caught sight of the *Laconia*, a flight of four-engine long-range B-24D bombers of the 343rd Bombardment Squadron flying from Brazil to the North African war zone had passed through Ascension Island. One of the planes developed a smoky engine problem, and the pilot, Lieutenant James Harden, decided to stay at Wideawake for repairs. It was a fateful decision for the young pilot.

CHAPTER 6

Sinking *Laconia*

SATURDAY, SEPTEMBER 12, 1942

As the night of September 12 closed in on the great old ship making her way slowly up the West African coast, few of her passengers anticipated trouble. Captain Sharp remained anxious about the smoke pouring from his ship and the fact he was alone in a vast sea that enemy submarines considered their hunting ground. He kept the ship on a strict zigzag regime during daylight hours and made the best time his ship could at night. With a little luck, they would all make it home safely. Avoiding the small talk usually found at the captain's table in the dining room, Sharp opted to eat alone at his desk. Leaving nothing to chance, he spent each night sleeping in his uniform near the Chart Room. He was never off duty.

Life jackets were the order of the day. Passengers and crew were instructed to either have one on at all times or else close by. But as with people everywhere, an increasing number of passengers became lax about this precaution and left their invaluable life-saving devices behind as the days and nights dragged on with no indication of danger. During the day people played shuffleboard on the deck or even a bit of tennis once a member of the crew remembered where the net was and hung it on a rear deck. Others lounged around and chatted, played cards, or engaged in whatever helped them pass the time.

Two days earlier the *Laconia*'s strict radio silence was broken by a message from the Admiralty. Captain Sharp received instructions to alter his course the following evening. The new heading was westerly, away from the African coast. This raised the possibility in his mind, and in the minds of the officers around him, that they were not going home after all, but perhaps heading toward North America or the West Indies.

The course change was fateful, for it brought that smoke trail within sight of U-156, making its way south toward the Cape Town area. Had the *Laconia*'s course not been altered, Hartenstein might never have been aware of the liner's progress in the opposite direction.

Life in the holds remained miserable. While the food and sanitation had improved a little, the Italians suffered from too many men in too small a space. They remained locked in the holds 22 hours out of each 24. They were brought up on deck in small numbers each day for exercise and the luxury of breathing clean fresh air for one hour in the morning and again in the evening. Some of them were detailed for chores aboard the ship, but for most, their fate was the dark airless hold of the huge ship.

On board the U-boat, Hartenstein spent the day keeping a keen eye on his prey. As he slowly drew closer, he realized that this was a ship of large tonnage, perhaps as large as 20,000 tons. If that were the case, sinking her would bring his total to over 100,000 tons, and earn him and his crew special recognition.

On board *Laconia*, Third Officer Buckingham completed his evening rounds, checking that the blackout rules were being followed and arranging for a few prisoners to find the comfort of the spare sick bay beds. He returned to the bridge at 7 P.M. and joined Captain Sharp in watching the last of the day's sun setting over the far western horizon. Sharp told Buckingham he estimated their location to be about 900 miles south of Freetown and 250 miles northeast of Ascension Island. A half hour later, Captain Sharp ordered the helm to stop zigzagging and to keep a steady course. He then gave Buckingham and Junior First Officer Hall-Luca permission to go to dinner. Both men headed for the dining room on "D" Deck, considered the officer's mess.

Unseen by either man, or the lookouts posted around the ship, the enemy submarine sat just below the surface a few miles to the east. She was keeping her distance, especially after watching the vessel's gun crews practice firing during the afternoon. These drills helped keep the guns in working order and the sailors assigned to them in practice. They also offered some entertainment to bored passengers. Hartenstein did not know if the gun crews were any good at their jobs, but he did not want to learn the hard way. Perhaps he was recalling the determination of the gun crew aboard the *San Eliseo*, whose firing came dangerously close to their target.

By 8 P.M., U-156 was on the surface a little over two miles east of the *Laconia*. Hartenstein gave the order to prepare two torpedoes for firing. He watched the ship moving ahead and judged her speed and distance for accurate targeting. At 8:04, he gave the order to fire the first torpedo. The second torpedo was fired 30 seconds later. The submarine then submerged to periscope depth. Hartenstein was still unsure what his target was, but he knew it was armed and he was not going to take any chances.

Every survivor of the *Laconia* explosions and sinking, and the nightmare that followed, recalled exactly where they were and what they were doing when the first torpedo hit the ship at 8:07 P.M.

Third Officer Buckingham left the dining room and headed for Cabin 17 on "A" Deck. A Royal Navy officer and his wife whom Buckingham had promised to visit briefly after dinner occupied the cabin. Just as the ship's officer raised his hand to knock on the door a violent explosion rocked the ship and almost threw him to the deck. The cabin door in front of him disintegrated and filled the air with gray dust. After the few seconds it took Buckingham to realize what had happened, he yelled over the noise of the explosion that the couple should immediately leave the cabin and go directly to their lifeboat station. They instantly did as ordered. Thirty seconds later the second torpedo struck as Buckingham headed for the bridge.

The ship rocked to port from the impact and explosion, then back to starboard. When the second torpedo hit she was thrown back to port again. She soon stopped rocking and began a gradual and irreversible tilt to starboard as the ocean poured in through the two holes blasted in her starboard side just below the waterline.

Jim McLoughlin, formerly of HMS *Valiant,* was heading down to "G" Deck to have dinner with Fred Eyres, the man in charge of the food supplies known as the pantry-man. Fred had been in the same position when Jim's father had been the first class steward, and Fred told Jim to join him for a meal anytime. Jim was hungry and looking forward to what he knew would be a great meal, when there was what he described as "a brain-numbing explosion."

McLoughlin explains what happened next: "The noise was crushing. I felt like I'd been punched in the head by a powerful fist of sound." He was lifted into the air, thrown backwards into the steel bulkhead, and dropped to the floor in a heap trying to catch his breath. Following a few seconds of shocked silence, all hell broke loose around him as people, mostly British soldiers who minutes earlier had been lounging around smoking and playing cards "without a care in the world," rushed to the stairs he had just descended. He started back up himself.

When Buckingham arrived at the bridge he found Captain Sharp out on the starboard wing leaning over the railing trying to access the damage caused by the two torpedoes. It looked very bad as the ship slowly rolled over toward her starboard and the water continued rushing in. A duty officer told him the captain had given the abandon ship order, but the communications system was out so they sent messengers to various parts of the ship to spread the word. The remaining officers on the bridge quickly left, heading for the boat deck to assist in getting as many lifeboats off safely as possible.

Captain Sharp reminded his third officer about the documents containing secret Admiralty codes in the safe. It was Buckingham's job to see they went into the water in their heavy weighted bags should the ship come under attack. With the help of the quartermaster, Buckingham dragged the heavy canvas bags through the bridge and onto the wing, where the two men lifted them over the rail and dropped them into the sea. The bags had perforations so water could easily fill them and weights to ensure German sailors who might board the sinking ship in search of the codes would not recover them. They would drop right to the ocean bottom.

Looking over the side, he could see the water was full of people struggling to swim away from the ship. He had to steel himself to his duty as he dropped the bags. "Whilst dropping the confidential mail overboard I knew it was falling among the people in the water, but this could not be avoided."

True to his Royal Navy training, Jim McLoughlin fought his way to the upper deck and toward the stern gun, where he had been assigned to augment the regular DEMS gun crew. All the while people were screaming for help or searching for loved ones in the mostly darkened spaces and on the open deck. In a few places, the emergency lights worked, but the ship was leaning over so far it was almost impossible to get a strong footing. As he made his way to the stern, people simply slid past him and were thrown into the ocean. Others in a state of desperation jumped into the water hoping to get away before the ship went down. He thought he heard fireworks mixed with the sounds emanating from the dying ship at one point; however, someone told him that the Polish guards and some British officers were firing at groups of Italian prisoners. Evidently, some of the POWs had broken out of their prisons and were attempting to wrest control of lifeboats containing women and children. With all the chaos and noise around him, he did not know what to believe, so he followed his trained instinct and headed toward the stern gun.

Once the confidential bags had been dumped into the sea, Buckingham headed toward the radio room to see if the operators had been able to send out distress signals. It did not look promising; he noticed that the main mast containing the radio antenna had toppled over and dropped onto the roof of the First Class Dinning Room, causing the roof to collapse. Luckily there were few, if any, passengers in the room.

Buckingham found it tough going. He had to go down two levels, then back past the funnel, and back up again. All the way, there were hundreds of screaming people fleeing for their lives who did not know where to go. All the while, the ship continued its gradual roll to starboard. Getting around was even more difficult due to the fact the ship was now not only leaning to the side, but she was beginning to go down by her bow. Items that were strapped down on the decks now broke loose and smashed against bulkheads, often crushing people in the process. The trip to the radio room proved without value. The wireless operators told the officer the mast had come down before they could send an emergency message.

They were only able to send a distress signal over the emergency radio, but with a range of less than 50 miles, it was unlikely anyone would hear it. There was little chance of anyone sending help.

Jan Derych went off duty at 8 P.M. He stripped off his uniform shirt and, carrying his life jacket, headed to the deck just outside the ballroom to watch a group of dolphins swimming around and jumping into the air. Less than 10 minutes after his arrival, "all hell broke loose." The torpedoes slammed into the ship and exploded, sending the huge vessel rocking violently back and forth as she sought her own equilibrium. Derych realized the ship was tilting over and he would soon be thrown into the sea, so he rushed through the ballroom toward the other side. The lights suddenly went out, and people began screaming and calling to one another. The angle of the ship and the waxed floor of the ballroom made it almost impossible to walk from one side of the room to the other, so most people attempted to crawl to what they hoped was safety. Some did make it to a doorway to which they clung, but most kept sliding back.

Outside, he joined with several crew members who were attempting to get as many lifeboats, rafts, and anything else that would float into the water. The crew had great difficulty lowering some of the boats, as the cables holding them were rusted and refused to budge. When they were unable to lower the boat nearest him, a crew member used a bayonet in an attempt to hack through the rusted hawser. "The navy had been so certain," said Derych, "that the *Laconia* would be safe, they had not had a practice drill for evacuating the ship in case of danger—which meant the lifeboats had not been checked and tested." In the panicked rush to abandon ship, some of the boats were lowered into the sea without the bungs inserted into the drain holes in their hulls. As a result, they quickly filled with water and sank. Several of the boats filled with passengers were lowered too quickly and slid along the hull of the ship, overturning and throwing people into the water or smashing them against the side of the ship. Many were killed or seriously injured.

Behind him, Derych heard men calling and screaming; some of the Italian prisoners had managed to crawl out of their prison through several air vent chutes about three feet in diameter. The chutes, usually vertical on the deck, were now nearly horizontal as the ship continued its inevitable roll. He helped several crew members rip the wire screening off the chutes to allow the prisoners to escape. The crew members with him, who by now had thrown anything that might float into the water, said their work was done and left the ship. Derych followed them over the side and into the water. Luckily, he was wearing his life vest, but he had failed to fasten the ties along each side. As a result, "the back cushion floated horizontally, while the front one was pushing my chin up." He knew instantly that he was in "deep, deep trouble." Then, to his amazement he felt "something come up underneath me, lifting me up long enough for me to grab the tapes and knot them as tight as I could under my arms. Suddenly I was back in the water, watching the creature swimming away and diving—it was a dolphin." He was grateful it had not been a shark.

From below decks, 17-year-old Albert Goode and a mate struggled against the growing list of the ship and the overwhelming smell of cord- ite from the two explosions. They attempted to make their way through the dark companionways toward an upper deck, but found the passage blocked by hundreds of Italian POWs, whose futile attempts to get to an upper deck were stopped by gunfire from above. Goode could not tell if Polish guards or British military personnel were shooting. Goode and his companion decided they had better return to their quarters to retrieve their life jackets for safety's sake. Along the way, they passed three crew members that had actually been killed by rivets that burst from the hull and bulkheads during the explosions.

The two became separated amidst the screaming people running in all directions looking for safety and survival. When Goode reached the boat deck, he saw that all the boats had been launched except for two that hung uselessly from their rusted cables. Seeing no alternative, he decided to jump off the side of the ship and attempt to catch one of the lifelines hang- ing from it. He missed the line nearest him and hit the water with such impact that he momentarily thought he would never surface again. Luck- ily, he rose and found himself very close to a Carley float (which was a lightweight raft that could be launched easily and quickly, and was used extensively in both World War I and World War II). He clung to it for dear life. He turned and looked back at his doomed ship.

When Jim McLoughlin arrived at the stern gun, he found John Hen- nessey and Peter Tinkler waiting for him. The officer in charge of the gun—a man they all liked very much, Lieutenant Tillie—told them it was useless to attempt to locate the U-boat in the dark, and anyway, that it was probably miles away by now. The men realized the stern of the ship was lifting out of the water, as the bow was going under, so they decided it was time to go. He recalled the navy's admonition to never abandon a ship in the direction it was turning, because you ran the chance of being caught under the ship as she turned over. He crawled his way to the port side, but found it was much too high to consider jumping. His only alter- native was to ignore the navy's advice. By now separated from his mates, McLoughlin jumped into the water on the starboard side and swam away as fast as he could.

Another survivor who jumped from the ship was Ernest Barnes of the Seventh Hussars. Despite his leg wound, he managed to swim to a life- boat. Unfortunately, one of the boat's occupants must have mistaken him for an Italian prisoner and gave him a whack on the head with his oar. Realizing their error, the others pulled Barnes into the boat. For a long time after he suffered from headaches, which he attributed to that blow to his head. But he had at least survived and was safely in a lifeboat.

Third Officer Buckingham fought his way back to the bridge one final time. He found a sad and tired-looking Captain Sharp reading a chart with the help of a flashlight. Buckingham explained the situation with the radio antenna, making it clear it was unlikely help was on the way. Looking at his third officer for the final time, Captain Sharp thanked him and told him to go to the boat deck and get off the doomed ship. That was the last Buckingham would see of his captain. He aided the ship's doctor in getting an injured passenger into one of the few remaining lifeboats, removed his jacket, and dove off the end of the ship.

George Fish, the ex-stoker from HMS *Enterprise,* had just cleaned up for the evening when he heard the muffled sound of the first torpedo's explosion. He immediately knew what had caused the thud "that was unmistakable to a sailor." The second explosion confirmed his worst fears: "We had been torpedoed." The lights went out and he began slowly working his way up four decks to a level from which he could escape the ship. He reports that everything was pandemonium; people were screaming, yelling, and pushing each other as they crammed the narrow and nearly pitch-black stairways in an effort to flee almost certain death. All the while, the ship itself screamed as metal crushed against metal and objects broke loose from their moorings and flung around.

By the time he reached the outside deck the ship was tilted so far that he was able to walk along the huge hull and step off into the water and swim away. Dressed in his white pajama top, underwear, overalls, and black socks, the water felt warm and inviting. His one fear was that the tiny wounds on his feet from crossing the barnacles that clung to the hull would begin bleeding and attract sharks. As he swam away, he spotted a large grate, approximately 12 feet by 4 feet, and managed to pull himself onto it.

RAF Sergeant George Stoneman was in his cabin with his wife, Ena, and five-year-old daughter, June, when the first torpedo hit the *Laconia.* The couple were preparing for a dance that evening held for sergeants and their ladies. Ena was pressing George's trousers as he stood by, patiently waiting. June was in her bunk looking at a book. George and Ena were anticipating the dance, which was planned for the ship's main dining hall. Years later Ena could clearly recall the hum of the ship and the feel of the iron in her hand as the cabin suddenly shuddered and everything went black. Her first thought was that she had done something with the iron to cause the blackout, perhaps by shorting the electrical system. Turning to her husband, she said, "Oh George, I've fused the lights."

George responded that the ship was sinking, for he could feel her leaning from the first blast, even though he had not heard it. He picked June up, grabbed Ena by the hand, and rushed out of the cabin. Once outside the cabin Ena knew George was correct. "Outside there was chaos, water was streaming down the passageway and there were people screaming and shouting." They fought their way to the boat deck, where George put his wife and daughter into a lifeboat about to be launched. He told them he was going back to help people who were trapped. As the lifeboat drifted away, Ena was sure she would never see her husband again. Thankfully, she was wrong. After helping load people into other undamaged lifeboats, George jumped into the water and swam as quickly as possible away from the ship. He grabbed a hold of a lifeboat and pulled himself aboard only to find Ena and June were in the same boat.

If the passengers and crew on the upper decks of the ship thought things were bad, they had no idea what was happening in the holds, where panic and terror swept through the prisoners. The first torpedo smashed through the hull and exploded inside the number 4 hold. No one knows for sure how many prisoners in that hold died almost instantly, but the number was at least 400. Any that did survive the blast were drowned in the seawater that immediately cascaded into the hold. The second torpedo exploded in the number 2 hold, killing virtually every man in it. The Italians in the adjoining holds panicked as the explosion broke through bulkheads. Water rushed in from all sides and the men crashed their bodies against the cell gates and called to be released. Eventually, some of the bars bent and broke under the pressure of the bodies pushed against them. Many prisoners died because of the crush, but eventually several hundred were able to free themselves from what they all knew was sure death. Then they were confronted with another potentially fatal situation.

Lieutenant Colonel Baldwin, who had worked so hard to improve conditions for the prisoners, was now evidently concerned that the terrified men rushing up the stairs from the holds would overwhelm the lifeboats containing women and children. He decided to hold them back with the assistance of several British Army officers who were wearing their side arms. He also rounded up a number of the Polish guards, who were armed with rifles but may not have actually had ammunition for their weapons, only bayonets. The men fired into the surging crowd, holding them back just long enough for the last lifeboat to get away. Baldwin and the others, joined by several hundred Italian soldiers, stepped off the sinking ship and swam as hard as possible to get away before the vessel went down and pulled them with her.

Two miles to starboard, Werner Hartenstein watched through the periscope in the rapidly disappearing light as the listing *Laconia* turned bow down amid the screeching of metal and escaping steam. The submarine's radio operator told Hartenstein that the vessel was sending a weak signal giving her name and the three-letter warning that she had been attacked by a U-boat—SSS. He ordered the man to jam the signal and watched as the ship's stern rose out of the water. She was preparing to go under by her bow. Years later David Chawe, a utility man aboard the *Laconia*, spoke of her as his "home." His eyes still filled with tears as he recalled watching her slip away beneath the water.

Hartenstein decided to move in among the lifeboats and debris to see if he could locate the ship's captain. Donitz had issued instructions that U-boat commanders should capture captains and other high-ranking officers whenever possible. Donitz knew that these experienced sailors were difficult to replace, and it made little sense to allow them to return to their countries and take command of new ships. He anticipated that a forced shortage of experienced captains would severely curtail Allied shipping.

The approaching rumbling hum of the U-boat's engines struck fear in the hearts of most of the *Laconia's* survivors. At least one lifeboat full of people quickly rowed away from the U-boat as she approached them. Standing in the conning tower of his boat, Hartenstein must have been amazed and somewhat dismayed by the sight around him. Hundreds of people were in lifeboats, on makeshift rafts, clinging to wreckage, or bobbing perilously in the water. Some called for help while others just stared silently at their attacker, probably waiting to be slaughtered.

The commander's meditation on the scene was suddenly broken when several members of the deck crew called to him that there were men in the water calling out *"Aiuto, Aiuto!"* the Italian word for help. He ordered the men brought aboard the boat. It was then the German sailors learned the ship they had sunk carried as many as 2,000 Italian soldiers as prisoners of war. The men pulled from the water told their allies that they had been mistreated, kept locked in the hold of the ship as she filled with seawater, and also that there were many women and children on board. The words spilled out so quickly from several excited mouths that the German sailor interpreting could barely keep up.

Suddenly all eyes were drawn to the massive ship as she groaned painfully into the night. She sat almost straight up as if being held by some invisible wire, then dropped out of view, replaced by a cloud of smoke and steam. The explosions of her boilers underwater could be felt in the U-boat—the final death throes of a mighty ship.

As the survivors watched, more and more people were pulled out of the water and onto the submarine's deck. For many, their initial fear evaporated as their attacker suddenly became their possible savior. Before he realized what was happening, Hartenstein found his U-boat surrounded by all those he had driven from their ship. They were on all sides calling for help. He told his men to keep pulling people out of the water, clearly indicating no distinction was to be made between Italians, Poles, or Brits. Some of those who came aboard the submarine had wounds inflicted by barracudas or possibly even sharks. The experienced sailors aboard the submarine and among the survivors knew that the large number of bodies floating in the water, many bleeding from wounds received in the explosions or while escaping, was bound to attract many of the man-eating predators.

Hartenstein watched all this with dismay. He knew once he had started pulling people from the water there was no turning back. Neither he nor his men could do such a thing. Finally, after several hours of this effort, and with his deck crammed with survivors, he decided he should inform Admiral Donitz of the situation. His message was brief and to the point: "Sunk by Hartenstein, British Laconia, Qu FF7721, 310deg. Unfortunately with 1,500 Italian POWs. 90 fished out of the water so far. Request orders."

It is likely that Hartenstein knew his man. Donitz might not be happy with the situation, but he was unlikely to order the U-boat commander to throw the people back in the water and get away from the scene before enemy ships and planes arrived. At this point, no one knew if the stricken ship's signals had been picked up by any Allied ship or land station. At that very moment, British warships could be speeding toward the site, and they would not look kindly on the German submarine that had caused so much death and pain.

Back in Paris, Donitz was awakened and informed of the coded signal received from U-156. His reaction was just as Hartenstein had expected. After debating the potential consequences of having one or more of his boats operating on the surface, vulnerable to attack, and the likely political impact with Germany's Italian ally over the sinking and a failure to rescue the Italian soldiers, he ordered other U-boats to the scene to help U-156. Without a doubt, he could not leave the Italian soldiers to their fate in the middle of the ocean after one of his boats had sunk their ship, even if they had been prisoners. They were now the responsibility of the Germans, and there was no way around it. Years after the war, the admiral told French historian Leonce Peillard, who wrote the first book devoted solely to the *Laconia* incident, that once Hartenstein had started the rescue operation, he could not order it stopped without doing damage to the morale of the men on the boat. He considered maintaining the high morale of men who volunteered to go to war in the small cramped submarines as one of his most important responsibilities. Not everyone on his staff agreed with his decision, but it was his alone to make. He had instructions sent to three U-boats: U-506, commanded by Wurdmann; U-507, commanded by Schacht; and the 1,700-ton supply boat U-459, commanded by Wilamowitz-Mollendorf. The three were told to head to square 7721 and Hartenstein at full speed. Wilamowitz-Mollendorf decided he was too far away to be of any help. Wurdmann and Schacht immediately set their courses for the tiny square in the ocean identified on their charts as 7721.

Meanwhile, early the next morning at U-boat headquarters Admiral Donitz decided to ask for help from his Italian counterpart, Rear-Admiral Angelo Parona, at Betasom. Parona immediately responded by ordering his nearest submarine, the *Comandante Cappellini,* to rush at full speed to the site of the sinking.

In Berlin, Admiral Raeder had the unenviable task of informing Hitler of what was going on at the site of the *Laconia* sinking. As he had already expressed his feelings concerning survivors of enemy ships, Hitler was not at all pleased. He told Raeder to limit the exposure of his U-boats as much as possible, and to get the operation over as quickly as he could. Raeder passed this message along to Donitz.

Someone suggested asking the Vichy French for assistance. Since virtually everyone claimed the idea, it is not certain who gets the credit. It was most likely Admiral Raeder. It was obvious to all that the submarines alone were not going to be able to accommodate the number of survivors. Larger ships were needed if the rescue was to be successful.

The primary contact between Germany and the French government responsible for the section of France not under full German occupation was the Franco-German Armistice Commission, a result of the armistice signed between the Germans and the remnants of the French Republic following their capitulation. The armistice, signed on June 22, 1940, established the border between German-occupied France and the area under French control and created the commission, which sat regularly in the quiet spa town of Wiesbaden. In a typical touch of irony probably instigated by German officials, the commission met at the luxurious Hotel Nassauer Hof, which had previously served as the French headquarters during France's occupation of the Rhineland resulting from the Treaty of Versailles. The Germans had reoccupied the territory on March 7, 1936. The headquarters of the French State—the term for unoccupied France—was in the town of Vichy. The government and its territory became known as Vichy France.

The French commissioners were informed of the *Laconia* incident. They were told of the Italians on board but may not have been informed of the large number of British because many Frenchmen were still angry over Churchill's decision to destroy much of the French Fleet to prevent it from falling into German hands. In any event, instructions reached the Vichy French authorities in North Africa to send several ships to aid in the rescue.

The commander of the French fleet at Dakar, Admiral Collinet, received the order just after 1 P.M. on Sunday, as he was preparing to leave his office for lunch. He quickly sent orders to Commander Francois Madelin to take his sloop, *Dumont-d'Urville*, to sea to meet the German submarines and take the *Laconia* survivors aboard his ship. Unfortunately, weather conditions distorted wireless communications, and the sloop did not set out for the rescue mission for another day.

Admiral Collinet soon realized that the small sloop would not be able to take aboard as many survivors as the U-boat had reported. He ordered two additional warships to join the rescue—a second sloop, the *Annamite*, and the much larger cruiser *Gloire*.

Meanwhile, communications between U-156 and U-boat headquarters had been rather extensive considering the enemy could also pick up the signals and use them to locate the submarine.

Donitz inquired if the ship had sent an SOS signal after being hit, to which Hartenstein answered truthfully that it had. That was not good. If the signal had been received by an Allied station, there could be several enemy ships currently underway who would love nothing better than to find a German submarine sitting on the surface, vulnerable to attack. At one point Hartenstein reported that he now had 193 people aboard his small boat. Conditions were obviously reaching the breaking point.

U-156 slowly maneuvered around the area, checking on people in lifeboats and pulling those still alive from the water. When someone was fished out of the sea, they were given dry clothes, while supplies lasted, or waited for theirs to be dried inside the sub. They were all given warm coffee or tea and something to eat. When recovered, the uninjured men were placed in several of the lifeboats that had room. The women and children were urged to stay aboard the U-boat, which most did.

With somewhere between 16 and 22 lifeboats successfully launched, and an uncounted number of rafts, as well as hundreds of people in the water, Hartenstein had his hands full just trying to pull them all together. Since many of those treading water had to fight off hungry barracudas that were feasting on the dead and living equally, he was glad to hear that three more submarines were on the way, and cheered later by the news that several surface ships would be joining the rescue.

Over the next few days the U-boat's kitchen worked around the clock, feeding the hundreds who were fished from the sea, soon placed into lifeboats, and replaced by additional victims pulled from the water. In addition, the sub was crowded with women, children, and injured men. One of the Italian prisoners was a doctor and looked after many of the latter. Hartenstein made his medicines and first aid supplies available to the doctor to use as he saw fit. German officers and crew gave up their sleeping places so *Laconia* survivors could use them.

As the wind and sea conspired to push lifeboats away, Hartenstein and his men kept circling the area, taking stragglers in tow and pulling them back together. Unknown to him, several boats had left the scene early on and headed east toward the African coast before they could discover that help was being offered. At least one writer described the U-boat's activities over the next few days, probably quite correctly, as resembling a sheep dog, rushing here and there trying to keep its ever-wandering charges together. However, in this case the charges—the people in the lifeboats—were not wandering off of their own accord, for most were either without the tools to control their boat's motion, or too weak to fight against the currents and wind.

Nursing Sister Doris Hawkins, who was on her way home after serving in Palestine, was with some difficulty pulled from the water into one of the rafts. She reports that during the day on Sunday she could periodically see the submarine moving about the area, and she and the men on the two rafts tied together were worried that they would be shot by the Germans. They feared, as she wrote, "a shower of machine-gun bullets." Instead, when U-156 approached them, they were thrown a line, pulled in close, and helped aboard. There were about 200 survivors on the submarine at the time, both below and on her crowded deck. Doris was surprised to learn that another 200 had been rescued earlier and, after being offered food and water, placed into lifeboats that still had room. Many of the lifeboats remained tied to the sub by long lines. She was more surprised when she was taken below to the officer's wardroom, where her clothes were dried and she was given "hot tea and coffee, black bread and butter, rusks [a biscuit] and jam."

Writing of the experience upon returning to England, Hawkins portrayed enemy sailors many of her fellow citizens did not recognize. "The Germans treated us with great kindness and respect the whole time; they were really sorry for our plight. The commandant was particularly charming and helpful; he could scarcely have done more had he been entertaining us in peace-time." One of her greatest surprises was that even after being given free rein of the submarine, she never heard a "Heil Hitler" once, and saw no swastikas. The only photo she saw of Hitler was one tucked away in "a small recess."

Werner Hartenstein may have been "charming and helpful," but he was also the commander of a submarine in wartime. Concerned about his boat's ability to quickly submerge should an enemy warship arrive, he decided to put the people on his deck into every available space in the lifeboats temporarily, and make a test dive. The lines attaching the lifeboats to the U-boat were untied, and the people on the deck, mostly men, were offloaded into the boats. The Germans explained that this was only a temporary measure. The dive was made successfully, the lifeboats rounded up, and the lines retied to the submarine. Once again, the deck of U-156 was crowded with the survivors of the *Laconia*.

For most of the survivors of the *Laconia*, the overnight hours from Saturday to Sunday had been a miserable experience. For many still in the water, it was deadly, as the barracudas and sharks continued feasting. Everyone was wet and cold. The lifeboat Tony Large had been able to board was missing its bung, but luckily one of the occupants picked up a piece of soft wood floating by and was able to carve a new one. Most of the boats leaked badly and required constant bailing. In some cases, the waterlogged wood swelled and sealed the openings, but in others, the bailing never ceased.

One of the most distressing things about being in a lifeboat, or worse, the water, aside from the discomfort and danger, is that you are low in the water and cannot see very far, and the feeling of isolation makes matters even worse. Third Officer Buckingham clung to a floating corpse for hours until he caught sight of a lifeboat and managed to swim to her. Its occupants pulled the very exhausted man aboard where he virtually collapsed from his exertions.

CHAPTER 7

A Message to the Enemy

Radio messages flew back and forth between U-156 and U-boat headquarters during the night. Most members of Donitz's senior staff were distressed by what was happening and that the admiral was sending additional U-boats to help. These boats were supposed to be sinking enemy ships, not rescuing people and leaving themselves open to attack.

Hartenstein was told help was on its way, but he suspected none of the submarines or surface vessels would arrive for several days. The situation around him had not improved. The German sailors passed out cold cream to people with bad sunburn, gave medical aid to the injured, and food and water to all, but they could not keep it up indefinitely. With supplies depleting rapidly, they were bound to run out, and the crew had grown exhausted by the constant rescue and care of survivors. Damaged lifeboats were brought aboard the U-boat and repaired as best as possible, then put back in the water to relieve the overcrowding on the sub's deck. The almost constant rotation of people moving from lifeboat to submarine and back again was taking a physical toll on the men. There was no indication that the crew disagreed with their commander's decision to help the survivors, but the job was much greater than they could have anticipated. Bodies and body parts in the water brought on regular forays by the barracudas and sharks.

In one message, Hartenstein reported he had 193 people from the *Laconia* on or inside his submarine. Hundreds more surrounded him. Lifeboats that either drifted away because they had inadvertently come untied, or were intentionally rowed in an ill-advised attempt to make the African coast, exacerbated Hartenstein's problems. The U-boat had to keep navigating the crowd of boats and rafts in an effort to keep them together for a practical recovery. There was also concern over trouble erupting in the boats, most of which were occupied by Italians and British, with a few Poles. Although there had been no clear indication of trouble, the German commander was worried about a possible retaliation by the POWs against their former captors.

Whether from frustration over the anticipated wait for assistance, or the declining condition of the people for whom he had assumed responsibility, Hartenstein took an unprecedented step. Early on Sunday morning he sent the following message, in English and on two open frequencies, seeking help from anyone, especially Allied ships that might be in the area: "If any ship will assist the wrecked Laconia crew, I will not attack her, provided I am not attacked by ship or aircraft. I have picked up 193 men." He then gave his position, and signed the message "German submarine."

It is possible that this message was received by at least one British listening station in Africa. Records are unclear on this point; it is also probable that anyone picking up the message would have interpreted it as a trap. The French at Dakar heard the signal and wondered what the Germans were up to.

Meanwhile, out in the ocean, Sunday passed into Monday. The burning sun baked the survivors during the day, and the hundreds that could not fit inside the submarine suffered from the cold temperatures during the night. Still more survivors were discovered clinging to bits of wreckage or simply floating around waiting for death to take them. The lookouts on U-156 kept a sharp eye out for approaching ships or aircraft. When the sun went down on Monday, the survivors huddled together in the lifeboats or on the deck of the submarine. Those lucky enough to have been given a blanket shared it with those closest to them, but there were just too many people and too few blankets. During all this, the submarine's cook worked night and day preparing soup and other foods for everyone.

Shortly before noon on Tuesday, September 15, one of the lookouts called to Hartenstein, who was sitting in the conning tower drinking coffee, partially dozing. He had not slept since this whole affair had begun. The man had spotted what appeared to be a ship on the horizon. Fear and hope mingled together in the hearts of all aboard the sub as they waited to see if the approaching vessel was there to help, or harm. It soon became apparent that it was a U-boat. It was, in fact, U-506.

Kapitänleutnant Erich Wurdemann did not record his first impressions as he pulled alongside Hartenstein's U-156, so one can only image what they were. The submarine had been turned into a refuge, not merely a rescue ship, for over 200 people. The deck was packed with over 100 men, many lacking all but the most essential bits of clothing; their skin was red from the sun and their faces sprouted rough beards. Everyone's hair was matted and thick from the salt water that regularly washed over the huddled survivors. Long lines that stretched from the rear of the submarine into the ocean were tied to over a dozen lifeboats rising and falling with the swells. Hundreds of survivors were in the lifeboats, all desperately in need of rescue.

When the U-boats were close enough for the commanders to hear each other, Wurdemann apologized to Hartenstein that he had taken so long to arrive. He then asked how many survivors were aboard U-156. Hartenstein replied that he had 233 people on board, about half of them Italians. Wurdemann responded that he would take all the Italians, thus keeping the British and Italians apart to ward off problems.

With the submarines lashed together, it took well over one hour to transfer the Italian soldiers to U-506. Most of these men had little or no experience of the sea and were terrified to leap from one pitching boat to the other. Slightly after 1 p.m., the transfer was completed and the submarines drew apart to search the area for additional survivors. When he compared the number of people under his care to the total on board *Laconia*, Hartenstein knew there had to be many more survivors beyond his visibility.

Between picking up lone survivors, and taking women, children, and injured men from lifeboats, Wurdemann had well over 200 people on board the following morning. He continued searching the area, keeping a sharp lookout for the expected French rescue ships.

A short time later, Korvettenkapitän Harro Schacht arrived. Before he even made visual contact with the other two U-boats, he began pulling people from the water and from damaged lifeboats. Everyone was brought on board, searched for possible weapons, and given a hot cup of soup. Injuries were treated and cigarettes were distributed to all who wanted to smoke.

Among those recovered from leaking lifeboats was the *Laconia*'s third officer, Thomas Buckingham. Some of the Italians, who the Germans could see were in worse physical condition than the British, must have complained to their allies regarding the treatment they had received as prisoners on the ship, especially after the torpedoes slammed into her. Several Italians recognized Buckingham as the officer who had made nightly visits to the holds searching out men to be brought to sickbay. Schacht had Buckingham brought to him in the conning tower. The U-boat commander questioned the British merchant officer about the treatment of the prisoners, and Buckingham assured him they had been treated humanely while aboard *Laconia*. Schacht said some of the Italians reported that the Polish guards had fired on them when they attempted to escape the sinking ship. Buckingham told him this was not possible since the Poles had not been issued ammunition for their weapons.

Schacht seemed satisfied for the time being, but told the British merchant officer that he intended to investigate the charges further. In the meantime, he said his job was to rescue as many people from the *Laconia* as possible without regard to nationality. He gave Buckingham binoculars, telling him to keep watch for swimmers and people clinging to wreckage.

He then returned to searching out and recovering victims of U-156's two torpedoes.

A few minutes before six that evening, Schacht radioed headquarters that he had 153 survivors on his boat. These included 149 Italians, 2 British women, an RAF officer, and Buckingham, the *Laconia*'s navigation officer. For some reason, he did not explain that he also had a large number of British survivors in a half dozen lifeboats in tow. Sensing there might be animosity between the Italians and their former captors, Schacht had separated them.

Meanwhile, northeast of the disaster that still covered the ocean surface with wreckage and bodies, the Italian submarine *Cappellini* raced to the scene at full surface speed. On the morning of Wednesday, September 16, Capitano di Corvetta Marco Revedin sighted a red sail ahead of him. Pulling alongside, he discovered it was a lifeboat from *Laconia*. The 50 people in the boat told Revedin they were all English. They had a compass, a map, and a radio transmitter operated by a pedal dynamo. The sub commander was surprised how well organized they appeared to be. Upon questioning, they explained that the only thing they needed was some water. He had his crew pass along a quantity of water bottles, throwing in several bottles of wine as a treat. Before resuming their journey, the lifeboat occupants told him to continue in the direction he was headed, as there were many more lifeboats in the water.

Three hours later the submarine approached another lifeboat with a red sail. This one was also full of English survivors, but included 18 women and 25 children, some quite young. He offered to take the women and children aboard, explaining there were too many men to fit into the submarine. The women declined, saying they desired to remain with their husbands. Revedin reported that one of the women, the Venetian wife of an Englishman, acted as a translator. When asked what they needed, they said blankets, something warm to eat or drink, a map, and a compass. Unable to give them blankets, he did give them a supply of warm broth, a barrel of drinking water, a quantity of biscuits and chocolates, and cigarettes. He explained that he had neither a map nor compass to give them, but he pointed out the direction they should follow to get to the nearest land. Before parting ways, the survivors told the Italian captain to keep on his present course where he would find several lifeboats full of his countrymen.

Later that evening he did find lifeboats full of Italian soldiers. Soon the *Cappellini* was crowded with survivors of all nationalities, and it struggled to keep a number of lifeboats together while Revedin awaited the arrival of the French ships.

The rescue attempts following the *Laconia* sinking went on for three days. They offered quite a scene if a viewer was high enough in the air to see a broad expanse of the South Atlantic Ocean. Four Axis submarines—three German and one Italian, usually far enough from each other to be out of sight of their comrades—were packed with Italian, British, and Polish survivors. Each submarine acted as a sheep dog trying to keep numerous lifeboats together to affect a transfer to the expected surface vessels. Each of the four struggled to provide medical care, food, water, and other help the survivors required. The commanders knew they could not continue much longer before their own limited supplies of food and water were exhausted. Everyone was anxious to see the French war ships on the horizon.

If things had remained as they were, the French ships would have met the Axis submarines and all the survivors of the *Laconia* would have been safely transferred and taken to North Africa. However, that was not to be.

CHAPTER 8

Air Attack

On Tuesday, September 15, the Americans at Wideawake Field received a somewhat garbled message from the British at Freetown reporting the *Laconia* sinking. The transmission reported the ship was carrying some 700 passengers and indicated another ship, the *Empire Haven*, was being diverted to look for survivors. There was no mention of the U-boat rescue effort, Hartenstein's attempt to declare the area a "neutral zone," or his request for Allied help. It is still unclear whether any of this information had reached Freetown, and if so, if it had been believed. Perhaps because of subsequent events, everyone concerned claimed they knew nothing of Hartenstein's broadcast. The information Ascension received was already three days old, and the position of the sinking provided to the Americans was wrong. In response, a flight of B-25 bombers made a futile search for survivors. In truth, the site of the sinking and the rescue efforts were beyond the distance these aircraft could travel and still return to base without running out of fuel.

Meanwhile, spread out across an expanse of the Atlantic, the four Axis submarines continued their humanitarian effort. Lifeboats were recovered and repaired where required, injuries were treated, and everyone was supplied with warm food and plenty of water. In the case of the *Cappellini*, bottles of wine were also distributed among those it had taken under its protection. In all cases, everyone was treated the same regardless of their nationality. It was a unique moment in an otherwise brutal war that left many survivors of the *Laconia* with high regard for the enemy sailors.

From the perspective of the Americans on Ascension Island, the mission they were given was simple. They were to locate victims from a sunken liner and give that position to the *Empire Haven*. If possible, they were to provide air cover for that ship during the rescue. They were completely unaware that enemy submarines had been rescuing those very same survivors for several days.

Adding tension, they were told that three Vichy French warships had left port and were headed their way. This information came once again through British sources because the American radio communications network had not yet been fully installed. The Allies suspected that many of the Vichy French Naval officers either harbored pro-Axis feelings or remained bitter against the British over the destruction of their fleet. Not knowing the ships were part of the growing rescue effort, the American troops on the island were put on alert to prepare for possible attack and perhaps a potential landing by enemy forces.

Late that evening a message was received indicating that the *Empire Haven* was to be joined by the armed merchantman HMS *Corinthian* in the search for survivors. The Americans were asked to provide air cover for them. Once again there was no mention of the U-boat activities. Lieutenant Harden was called to First Composite Squadron headquarters, along with his navigator, Lieutenant Jerome Perlman, and bombardier, Lieutenant Edgar Kellar. Harden was informed the squadron was taking temporary command of his aircraft and its crew. Their orders were to take off the following morning with a full load of bombs and depth charges and provide the cover the British had requested. The crew was to keep a sharp lookout for U-boats. It was suspected, in some cases fully justified, that U-boats stayed near the site of a sunken vessel waiting for rescue ships as new targets.

At 7 A.M. the following morning, Wednesday, September 16, Harden's B-24 lifted off from Wideawake Field and headed north-northeast. It was a clear morning with plenty of visibility. Two and one-half hours later the Americans caught sight of a U-boat towing several lifeboats. It appeared to be headed toward two other lifeboats.

On board U-156, a lookout heard the sound of the approaching aircraft and gave the alarm. Hartenstein must have hoped the plane was coming in response to the message for help he had sent days earlier. He had prepared for just such an eventuality by having a large red cross sewn onto a six-foot-square piece of white cloth. As the plane approached, he ordered the cloth spread across the large deck gun. He then told everyone on the deck, which was crowded with survivors, to move away from the homemade flag so it could be seen. To his gunners, who were prepared to operate the anti-aircraft guns, he gave instructions to lie down out of sight. He made every effort possible to show the approaching pilot his peaceful and humanitarian intentions.

As the plane approached and the noise from its four engines became deafening, people in the lifeboats waved and shouted to what they believed their saviors. Hartenstein stared at the plane through his binoculars. He saw it was a Liberator, and clearly saw its American markings. He expected the Americans were sending help.

His efforts were not in vain. Lieutenant Harden circled around about 250 feet above the scene. He clearly saw the Red Cross flag, the many people crowded on the submarine's deck, and the line of at least four packed lifeboats it was towing behind it. He realized the U-boat was doing something very unusual, and it looked to be asking for his help. He reports that he radioed the submarine to identify its nationality, but received no reply. At about the same time, Hartenstein ordered his signalman to ask the pilot if help was on the way. Unfortunately, no one aboard the bomber could read the signal lamp's message. The aircraft just kept circling above. Fearing the message might not have been understood, an RAF officer, believed to be Wing Commander Blackburn, asked Hartenstein for permission to communicate with the Americans. The German gave it. Using Morse code, Blackburn signaled that he was an RAF officer and the U-boat had rescued the survivors of the *Laconia,* including many women and children. There was no response.

After many anxious minutes, Harden turned his bomber to the southwest to get within radio range of Ascension Island. Once he was able to establish contact, he reported what he had witnessed, including the lifeboats and the Red Cross flag, and asked for orders. It is not clear if he informed the island's radio operator that he believed the U-boat was asking for help with several hundred people it had rescued.

Aboard U-156 and the lifeboats, people's spirits were raised. They knew the aircraft could not land in the ocean to help them, but they also knew it could call on ships in the area to relieve the U-boat of its burden and take the survivors to safety. This was what they expected.

At Wideawake Field, Captain Richardson called in his superior officer, Colonel Ronin, and another officer to discuss Harden's report. They agreed it was obviously an enemy submarine Harden had seen, and should be destroyed if possible. However, there was the Red Cross flag and all those people on the sub and in the lifeboats. Who were they? Were they survivors from an Allied or Axis ship? There was no way they could know.

Meanwhile, Harden, who was flying a tight pattern out of range of the U-boat, became anxious about his fuel supply. If he waited much longer, he might not get back to the island. He radioed again for a decision, explaining his predicament. Finally, the men on Ascension Island made their decision, if somewhat reluctantly. Their primary mission was to safeguard Allied shipping through the area. U-boats were taking a high toll on ships, cargoes, and crews, and here was an opportunity to sink one. If they succeeded it might prevent the sinking of any number of Allied ships. Richardson gave Harden a four word order: "Sink sub at once!"

The B-24 turned and headed back northeast.

It had been about 30 minutes since the American plane had flown off. Everyone was hoping to soon see a rescue ship. Instead, they watched as the plane flew in a great arc, circling in toward them. Hartenstein, worried perhaps that this was not a good sign, watched the lower body of the plane and the bomb bay doors. To his horror, they opened. Dropping down from about 250 feet, Harden released two bombs. They both missed the target, causing huge gushers of water to wash over those standing on the deck of the submarine. The explosions told it all; the aircraft was attempting to sink the U-boat, without regard for the people it had rescued from the *Laconia*.

Hartenstein had stationed a man on the stern of the sub with an axe for just such an occurrence. He signaled the man to cut the line linking the U-boat to the lifeboats in tow. When the line split from the impact of the axe, the boats, all overloaded with people, began to drift and collide with each other.

As the plane circled around again for a second run, Hartenstein ordered evasive maneuvers. The first two depth charges had been released too soon, and the second too late, to strike the sub, but they fell among the lifeboats. One boat, full of Italian soldiers, was blown to pieces. A second lifeboat was overturned and its bottom ripped out. Dozens of people from the *Laconia* died in this attack. The aircraft once again flew a great arc around the target and headed in for another attack. An officer called to Hartenstein, requesting that the anti-aircraft guns shoot the offender down, but the commander refused.

The *Laconia* survivors in the lifeboats—British, Italians, and Poles alike—looked in disbelief at what was happening. Some were stunned into silence while others raised their fists to the airplane and shouted obscenities at it and its crew.

On its third pass, Harden's plane came closer to damaging the U-boat. Once again, it dropped two depth charges. One missed entirely, but the other fell close enough to U-156 that it exploded beneath her, causing the boat to rise out of the water and splash back down. Almost immediately, damage reports were received in the conning tower. The boat was taking on water.

Hartenstein watched as the enemy bomber, evidently having exhausted its bomb load, flew off to the southwest. He ordered his submarine to turn around and head back to the remaining lifeboats. Already overcrowded, they were pulling the few survivors from the wrecked lifeboats aboard. The submarine stopped as close to the lifeboats as it could, and the commander ordered all British survivors on his U-boat to jump overboard. There were approximately 110 people on and in the U-boat. The British personnel on deck jumped into the shark-infested water while those below, including women and children, climbed quietly and quickly up through the hatches and jumped overboard. Everyone realized the commander had no choice. He had risked his life and the lives of his crew in this rescue effort, but now he had to get his submarine out of the area before another attack.

Hartenstein first thought he would keep the Italians on board, since they were, after all, German allies. Then came a report from below that gas was leaking from the batteries. He gave the order for the crew to put on their gas masks. Now the Italians had to go, since there was only enough protective gear for the crew.

With all the passengers overboard, the U-boat headed away in a westerly direction. More than 100 people were forced overboard because of the attack. Very few of them survived. On closer inspection, the damage to the submarine proved to be less than was first reported, which is not unusual in those circumstances. The crew worked diligently to get their U-boat back in shape so they could continue what they had been sent to do—sink enemy ships.

As for the Americans, they evidently believed they successfully sank the U-boat, for this is what they reported when they returned to Wideawake Field. Their report included a description of the submarine turning over in the water and several crew members clinging to wreckage or swimming toward the lifeboats.

After a few hours, the submarine was repaired sufficiently to return to its original mission. Hartenstein sent Donitz a message describing what had happened. The admiral responded that he should take no further part in the "salvage operation." He was told to report on his fuel and torpedo supply. Donitz, keenly aware that the U-boat had been feeding several hundred people for the last few days, also wanted a report on what provisions Hartenstein had left.

Meanwhile, at U-boat headquarters, there was a dispute over what to do about U-506 and U-507. Some officers wanted them to also cease their rescue efforts lest they too come under attack. Donitz, however, declared that once a mission was begun it had to be completed. The French ships were due the following day, and this mission could yet be ended successfully. Orders were sent to Schacht and Wurdemann to be on extra alert concerning enemy air activity and not to rely on a Red Cross flag for protection. They were told to transfer all non-Italians to the lifeboats and be prepared to dive on a moment's notice.

On Thursday morning, Harden and his B-24 crew returned to the scene to look for survivors. The two British merchant ships were approaching the area and would require instructions on the location of the lifeboats. The bomber crew could not believe their luck when they spotted another U-boat sailing along on the surface. This was U-506, with well over 100 survivors aboard. The boat was on the alert and quickly dove as the bomber swept down on it and released some of its weapons. It was a narrow escape, but the bombs and depth charges did not damage the submarine. The Americans claimed a "possible sinking" of an enemy submarine.

That same day the French ships arrived and began taking people off the submarines and out of lifeboats. They cruised the area for several days, pulling stranded people out of the water and off pieces of wreckage until they were satisfied that they had recovered all survivors. The *Cappellini*, which had never actually encountered the U-boats, turned the people it had taken aboard over to the French, with the exception of several British officers who were taken prisoner.

The cruiser *Gloire* returned to Dakar with over 1,000 survivors. A few days later, the two sloops also returned with several hundred more. Most of the survivors were taken to a POW camp from which they were liberated a few weeks later by American troops.

Two lifeboats missed the rendezvous with the French and set off toward the African coast, some 800 miles away. One boat made land 26 days later, but only 16 of its original 68 passengers remained alive. The second boat, which had started its journey with 52 survivors, was discovered by a British trawler after 40 days. Only four of its passengers remained alive.

In all, about 1,600 people lost their lives as a result of the *Laconia* sinking. Approximately 1,000 were Italian prisoners of war. Many died because of the Germans' attack, but others survived because of the Germans' reaction afterward. Others died because of the American bombing. Scores of survivors remained bitter about that for the rest of their lives. Years later, some of those who had survived because of Hartenstein's actions continued to express their appreciation. Tony Large, a Royal Navy passenger on the *Laconia*, told interviewers, "I have nothing but admiration for what he did." Another Royal Navy passenger, Harry Gibbons, called him "A great fellow. I am sorry he's dead."

The events of Wednesday, September 16, were catastrophic for the survivors of the sunken ship, as well as the German sailors aboard U-156. They would also have an impact on the future behavior of the commanders of the U-boat war, and result in war crimes charges against Admiral Donitz.

CHAPTER 9

Aftermath

By the time the *Laconia* rescue mission had been completed, and all known survivors were safely aboard one of the French warships or making their way toward the African coast in a lifeboat, Donitz was angry and frustrated. He had allowed his boats to engage in the rescue regardless of Hitler's opposition to such actions. Hitler had expressed his feelings on the matter as early as January 2, 1942, at a meeting with the Japanese Ambassador, Hiroshi Oshima. Hitler told Oshima, "I must give the order that since foreign seamen cannot be taken prisoner . . . the U-boats are to surface after torpedoing and shoot up the lifeboats." He explained that the United States could build as many ships as she wanted, but a high death rate among merchant seamen would mean fewer and fewer men would be willing to serve aboard those ships. Oshima expressed his full agreement with this statement.

Donitz later denied any knowledge of this conversation, which is entirely possible. Hitler is believed to have approached the subject again at a May 14, 1942, meeting with Donitz and Grand Admiral Raeder. Although there is no surviving record of the discussion, many believe Hitler asked Donitz to reduce the number of survivors from enemy merchant ships that had been sunk by U-boats. Donitz avoided the issue of killing men in the water by focusing on improved torpedoes that would send a ship to the bottom more quickly, giving crews less time to get away. That seemed to mollify Hitler somewhat, at least for the time being.

In the *Laconia* sinking, Donitz had not only approved rescuing survivors—Italian allies, as well as enemy British and Poles—but he had also sent two more U-boats to help. In addition to U-156, U-506, and U-507, he had requested the assistance of an Italian submarine and asked the French to send surface ships to pick up survivors. Disapproval of the entire rescue effort, carried out in disagreement with several members of his own staff, was now exacerbated by the fact an Allied plane had bombed the scene. The incident had spun out of control. He now decided to remove the option to aid survivors and banned such attempts entirely. He had come to believe that eventually such humanitarian gestures would cost the lives of U-boat crews and result in the loss of the boats themselves. They had been lucky this time that the bombs had been poorly placed, with the lives of *Laconia* survivors the only cost.

As a result, on September 17, once the *Laconia* mission had neared completion, and again on September 20, he sent a message to all U-boat commanders that later became known as the Laconia Order.

1. Every attempt to save survivors of sunken ships, also the fishing up of men and putting them in lifeboats, the setup right of overturned lifeboats, the handing over of food and water have to be discontinued. These rescues contradict the primary demands of warfare esp. the destruction of enemy ships and their crews.

2. The orders concerning the bringing in of skippers and chief engineers stay in effect.

3. Survivors are only to rescue, if their statements are important for the boat.

4. Stay hard. Don't forget, that the enemy didn't take any regard for women and children when bombarding German towns.

Donitz faced Hitler's wrath over the *Laconia* affair on September 28 at a Berlin meeting. Hitler told his submarine force commander that it was "nonsense" to offer survivors food, water, and sailing instructions. He then ordered Donitz to order his U-boat commanders to kill all survivors from crews of sunken ships, "even if the crews are in lifeboats." To his everlasting credit, Donitz refused. He pled that U-boat crews were volunteers fighting what they believed was an honorable war and to kill survivors in lifeboats would undermine their morale. He knew his U-boat crews and officers were not like the SS units that killed civilians by the thousands. They were basically German sailors; most wanted to conduct themselves according to the traditions of the sea, which included aiding shipwrecked people, enemy or not.

An additional factor that probably influenced the future decisions of U-boat commanders, perhaps even more than the Laconia Order, was the likelihood that many had overheard Hartenstein's transmissions with U-boat headquarters. They knew firsthand that an Allied aircraft had bombed him while he was trying to help Allied survivors. There was definitely a lesson to be learned from that.

What were the effects of the experiences of U-156, U-506, and U-507 while rescuing survivors of the *Laconia*, as well as the Laconia Order? The ramifications for the U-boat commanders and the survivors of sunken ships are difficult to judge. As for Donitz himself, he was to pay a severe price for issuing the order. By late 1942, Allied air power was roaming farther and farther into the Atlantic Ocean, making it increasingly difficult for German submarines to be on the surface, especially during daylight hours.

During the earlier phase of the war, when land-based aircraft were limited in both scope and range, a submarine in mid-ocean need only keep a sharp lookout along the horizon for telltale signs of an approaching ship—rising smoke, or even a warship's superstructure. These signals generally gave a U-boat enough time to dive for safety. However, with airplanes now faster and able to fly longer distances they could very quickly sweep down from behind cloud cover or out of the bright sun and be above a vulnerable surfaced submarine in seconds. The rising number of U-boats sunk by aircraft as the war dragged on attests to the reality of the fear of death from the sky among U-boat sailors.

In his monumental history of the U-boat war, Clair Blair emphasizes the changing environment for U-boats in the Atlantic war zone by dividing his history into two volumes. The first, starting in 1939 and ending in August 1942, is titled *The Hunters*. The second volume, beginning with September 1942 and running through the end of the war, is titled *The Hunted*. Blair saw the autumn of 1942 as the pivotal turning point for the U-boats and their war. America had entered the war and was building ships—both merchant and naval—faster than the Germans could sink them. As an example, he points out that for the three years of the war prior to August 1942, German submarine forces sank a total gross tonnage of 9.3 million Allied ships. While that may appear an impressive performance, later in the war American shipyards alone were constructing in excess of six million gross tons of new merchant ships per year. Reality proved Hitler correct; his navy could not sink ships fast enough to stop their overall numbers from increasing. However, he hoped to be able to reduce Allied shipping activity if men were sufficiently fearful and refused to go aboard. Fortunately for the Allies, this did not happen. It is probably due, at least in part, to U-boats not living up to Allied propaganda and Hitler's wishes. As a matter of course, they did not kill survivors from the ships they sank.

The many technological advances used by the Allies against the U-boats confounded the German effort. In addition to the rapid construction of long-range aircraft, they developed direction-finding equipment originally confined to land but quickly miniaturized for installation aboard warships. Improvements and miniaturization of radar aided both ASW (Anti-Submarine Warfare) ships and convoy escorts in locating and attacking U-boats.

Code breaking was another major deterrent to German progress. German military codes were broken early in the war, and despite some periodic changes made by the Germans, Allied code breakers were able to read U-boat messages on a regular basis. This helped keep track of individual U-boat activities and determine their locations.

Around the time of the sinking of the *Laconia*, the war was turning against the U-boats. Merely running on the surface, which was required to recharge a submarine's batteries, became problematic, even at night. Groups of U-boats had previously been able to cross the ocean moving mostly on the surface. This time- and cost-effective method had become a luxury many paid for with their lives. According to Blair, by early fall 1942, well over 1,000 aircraft of varying types and ranges were being used for the express purpose of hunting and destroying U-boats. The number of U-boats sent to the bottom by newly developed depth charges increased rapidly.

A stunning example of new technologies and the danger of being caught on the surface combining to cause the destruction of a U-boat is demonstrated by the sinking of the IXD2 U-boat U-197 on August 20, 1943. U-197 was Korvettenkapitän Robert Bartels's second U-boat. Earlier in the war, he had been in command of U-561, a VIIC boat, and had sunk or damaged six enemy vessels. Since taking over U-197 on May 20, 1942, Bartels had managed to sink only three ships and severely damage a fourth, the American Liberty Ship *William Ellery*. Despite a 450-foot hole in her port side, the Liberty Ship managed to limp into the Durban port for repairs.

After this disappointing performance, U-197 rendezvoused with U-181 several hundred miles south-southeast of Madagascar in the Indian Ocean. The meeting was scheduled for August 17; its primary purpose was for Bartels to pass along a new set of keys for U-181's transmission-coding device, the Enigma machine. The rendezvous actually took place early on Thursday morning, August 19.

Bartels gave Korvettenkapitän Wolfgang Luth a set of keys for his boat and a second set to pass along to Eitel-Friedrich Kentrat in U-196. Luth told Bartels he had seen several enemy merchant ships sailing without escorts, but had not taken action since he had no torpedoes left. Bartels said he would stay in the area and search for them.

Unknown to the German commanders, these radio transmissions were intercepted and decoded by a South African station. Using the information concerning the rendezvous and subsequent transmissions, South African intelligence officers were able to track the continued progress of U-197 using Direction Finding D/F equipment. Shortly after 7 P.M. on the day of the meeting, the South Africans deduced where U-197 would be the following day.

The next morning Royal Air Force Flight-Lieutenant O. Barnett took off in his American-made Catalina Patrol Bomber, equipped with machine guns and depth charges. At 1:10 that afternoon, Barnett caught sight of the U-boat approximately 100 miles south of Madagascar. With his naked eye, he had first seen a large white cap in the distance. Using his binoculars, he identified the submarine and estimated her speed at 10 knots. She was heading east, away from the African coast.

Barnett circled his plane to approach his target from the side, and dropped his altitude to about 50 feet to better aim both machine guns and shallow set depth charges. At the last minute, Bartels turned his boat to face the oncoming aircraft and opened fire with his anti-aircraft guns. The airplane and the submarine exchanged a barrage of gunfire as the plane passed overhead. Barnett released his full compliment of six depth charges, but all missed their narrow target.

The gunfight between aircraft and U-boat continued for about 30 minutes as the plane kept circling. Flight-Lieutenant Barnett could see that although his depth charges had failed to strike the boat, his machine gun fire was having results. The U-boat began to list to one side, indicating her hull had been pierced by the Catalina's shells. She appeared to be taking on water. The submarine was also beginning to leave a rapidly widening oil slick in her wake.

At 1:45, Korvettenkapitän Bartels called his men inside the boat and ordered a crash dive. Although it is unclear what was going on inside the U-boat, it is probable that the engines had received some damage and the sailors could not stop the inrushing water, for at 2:23 she sprung back to the surface. The men inside the submarine rushed onto the deck and began firing their guns at the enemy aircraft. A short time later, U-197 sent a distress signal to the other boats operating in the area that she was under aircraft attack and "unable to submerge."

Having expended his ammunition, Barnett dropped several smoke flares hoping a second search plane, piloted by Flight Officer C. E. Robin, would investigate. He continued to circle the area, keeping out of range of the U-boat's guns.

A few minutes after 5 P.M., Robin appeared and made two unsuccessful runs, attempting to straddle the submarine at its most vulnerable position. Each time, Bartels was able to turn toward the new attacker and open fire. Finally, on the third attempt, Robin did straddle the boat from 75 feet, dropping six depth charges. The U-boat blew apart almost immediately, throwing debris high into the air, and quickly sank. It left a collection of debris floating in a large oil slick on the surface. The two Catalina aircraft remained at the site for about 30 minutes, watching for survivors, but none appeared. They returned to their base.

After sinking a ship, a U-boat commander was inclined to surface and ask survivors the ship's name, cargo, and destination so he could make an accurate report. However, this practice became extremely dangerous as it left the boat vulnerable to a sudden air attack. The commander also might be faced with problems that outweighed the benefits of such information, such as seriously injured survivors, or people in lifeboats with little or no supplies and in desperate need of assistance. Many commanders appear to have adopted a policy to move out of the area rather than face turning down requests for help.

One week after sinking *Laconia,* and not far from that location, Hartenstein demonstrated very clearly that neither the Laconia Order, nor his experience during the incident, were about to change his behavior toward stranded seamen. On Saturday, September 19, 1942, U-156 sank the 4,745-ton British freighter *Quebec City.* The ship had sailed from Alexandria, Egypt, with a cargo of Egyptian cotton and cottonseed destined for England on August 6, 1942. She had steamed unescorted down the Suez Canal, through the Red Sea, and along the east coast of Africa to Cape Town. At Cape Town she refueled and made ready for the highly dangerous run north along the African west coast toward home, once again without escort. Her instructions were to make all possible haste for Freetown, where she would join a convoy under the protection of military escorts for the final leg of the journey. David C. Jones, an 18-year-old cadet officer, served as part of the gun crew for the *Quebec City's* stern gun, a four-inch Mark 5. The ship had four additional weapons for its own defense—two anti-aircraft guns mounted on the boat deck and one on each side of the bridge. Jones's assigned duties included being the "cordite man" for the larger stern gun. This entailed carrying a heavy leather pouch of cordite charge and inserting it behind the shell in the gun's breach.

Because of numerous U-boat sightings nearer the coast, Captain William Caradoc Thomas received a change of instructions while at sea. Instead of sailing *Quebec City* between Africa and St. Helena and Ascension Island, he was to take his ship farther west in the Atlantic and pass around both islands before turning back toward the east for Freetown. He was to continue zigzagging during the day and running dark at full speed at night. Jones reports that they could just barely see St. Helena, some 20 miles away, through the heavy rainsqualls off their starboard beam.

The torpedo fired from U-156 struck near the boiler room of *Quebec City* at 3:46 P.M., ripping a large hole in the ship. Water rushed in so rapidly there was not enough time to close the watertight doors leading to the engine room, which swiftly filled with seawater. The ship quickly began to list to starboard. Jones was in the cadet officers' bathroom when the explosion occurred. Finding the door jammed, he squeezed through the only available exit, a porthole, gripping his life jacket in his hand.

After grappling with the usual problems trying to launch lifeboats from a listing ship, 41 members of the crew of 45 successfully rowed away from the still-floating *Quebec City.* A short time later the periscope of the U-boat that had torpedoed their ship came into view and circled the area before the submarine surfaced. The men in the boats were apprehensive, having been indoctrinated with propaganda that German U-boat crews killed the survivors of ships they sank.

When the submarine surfaced, its two gun crews rushed to their weapons and made them ready for action. Other crew members appeared with automatic weapons, and two lookouts on the conning tower scanned the horizon and the sky for potential danger. Between the lookouts was the boat's commander, Werner Hartenstein. Jones described him as "a tall, military figure," with gold braid on his cap peak.

In English, the clarity of which surprised his victims, Hartenstein instructed the crew of the *Quebec City* to bring their boats alongside to be tied to the submarine. Hartenstein asked if the ship's master was aboard one of the boats. Captain Thomas stood up and gave his rank. The German commander then surprised them all by apologizing for the necessity of sinking their ship. It was war and there was not much else to be done.

Captain Thomas answered the usual questions concerning the name of his ship, her nationality, and her cargo and destination. This was followed by a further surprise for the British seamen. The German commander explained that he would have liked to tow their lifeboats at least some distance toward the African coast, but that an Allied aircraft had recently attacked him while he tried to save the survivors from another ship. He asked Thomas if he would prefer to head toward the coast, some 1,200 miles to the east, or south toward Ascension Island, which was much closer but more difficult to see from the level of a lifeboat. Captain Thomas knew the odds of finding the island were slim and opted for the coast. Thomas was brought aboard the U-boat to confer with Hartenstein about the planned lifeboat voyage. This accomplished, the submarine and lifeboats parted company.

During their voyage, the lifeboats became separated, each making its own way east. A passing British destroyer found one. After 14 days at sea, the second lifeboat, with Jones on board, made landfall near a small fishing village in Liberia. A short time later, they were picked up by another British vessel.

The survivors attributed their successful voyage at least in part to the detailed instructions given by the U-boat commander, who had shown the freighter's master, Captain Thomas, their current location and the distance to Cape Palmas on the southern tip of Liberia, the closest location on the African coast. The German had warned Thomas to be wary of the powerful southeasterly currents, which could drive their boat south of Cape Palmas and into the Gulf of Benin. This could mean an additional thousand miles of sailing to reach the coastlines of Nigeria and the Cameroons.

Korvettenkapitän Karl-Friedrich Merten also put his own humanity ahead of orders. Merten, whom we encountered in Chapter 2, commanded U-68, an IXC boat. At 8:30 p.m. on the evening of Friday, November 6, 1942, U-68 fired the first of two torpedoes into the side of the 8,034-ton British passenger liner *City of Cairo*.

Built in 1915 for Ellerman Lines Ltd of London, she was a single-screw coal burner. As a small passenger ship with Edwardian furnishings, she had had an undistinguished career.

The ship left Bombay, India, on October 1, 1942, and sailed south to two stops in South Africa. The first was Durban, followed by Cape Town. She departed Cape Town at 6 A.M. on Sunday, November 1. On board were slightly less than 300 persons. These included 155 members of the crew, a mix of Europeans and Indians. The latter, recruited in large numbers to serve aboard British ships, were known as Lascars. In addition, 48 Lascars were traveling to England to serve aboard newly constructed ships. Finally, there were 98 passengers, including 28 women and 19 children. Several of the women had been widowed by the war in the Far East and were returning home to pick up the pieces of their lives. Among them was 24-year-old Dulcie Kendall. Dulcie's husband had been a railroad engineer working on extending the Burma Railway into China. He had contracted cerebral malaria and died while fleeing advancing Japanese forces. She was taking her four-year-old son, Colin, home.

In the hold of the *City of Cairo* were over 7,400 tons of cargo, including timber, pig iron, manganese ore, cotton, and wool. Also in the hold was a cargo brought to the Bombay dock in a convoy of heavy army trucks escorted by many police officers and armed soldiers. The dockworkers, mostly Chinese coolies, had unloaded the 2,000 black wooden boxes and placed them into cargo nets. The cranes had lifted the nets and loaded the secret cargo into the ship. It was later revealed that the boxes contained silver rupees. It is believed there were 3¼ million ounces of silver coin.

At the time she was attacked, the ship was making for the Brazilian port of Pernambuco (today called Recife). Forty-six-year-old Captain William Rogerson, master of the *City of Cairo*, estimated he would arrive on or about November 16. Although a straight route meant a 3,600-mile journey, the requirement to zigzag during daylight hours would add an extra 400 miles and additional time to the trip.

When the first torpedo hit, most of the passengers were engaged in playing bridge or other social activities. Ted Elliot was a former navigating officer aboard the Capetown-class light cruiser HMS *Carlisle* and was heading to New Brunswick for posting as the navigating officer of another Royal Navy warship. Another passenger, Tom Parkinson, had joined Elliot for an after-dinner drink in the ship's lounge. The two knew immediately what had happened when they heard and felt what Elliot described as an "almighty crack." Despite the danger, the men headed to their respective cabins to retrieve their money before leaving the ship. Both survived the sinking and the long ordeal before being rescued, and they remained the closest of friends for the rest of their lives.

Dulcie Kendall was just finishing dinner with a companion, Freda Bullen, when the explosion nearly threw them out of their chairs. The lights went out, and Dulcie grabbed the life jacket she had placed over the back of her chair and began running down the corridor to her cabin. Once there, she recovered her flashlight and found Colin sitting in his bunk rubbing his eyes, still half-asleep. With the help of a fellow passenger, who carried Colin, they made it into a lifeboat.

Twenty minutes after firing the first torpedo, U-68 fired a second, finally sending the *City of Cairo* slowly down to her demise. Her chief radio officer, Harry Peever, died in the second attack. He was one of only two crew members lost in the sinking. Peever had ignored Captain Rogerson's abandon ship order, preferring to heroically remain at his post sending a distress signal stating the ship's position and that there were many women and children aboard. Inside the submarine, Merten heard the signal and responded to it as if he were from the Walvis Bay station in South Africa, hoping to trick the radio operator into believing a friendly base had received his signal and to stop broadcasting. The German commander was shocked that the ship was carrying so many civilians, especially women and children. He later commented that after listening to the distress signal he found it "difficult to comprehend the irresponsibility of the Allied authorities" in sending a ship with women and children aboard out of Cape Town without a naval escort when "it was well known that a pack of submarines" were operating in the area.

The submarine approached the lifeboats soon after the ship went down. Later reports stated that the U-boat surfaced among the lifeboats, but this was not the case. As Merten himself pointed out, U-68 had surfaced long before firing the first torpedo, since "at that period there was no possibility whatsoever of attacking a ship on a dark night by periscope in a submerged state." In his nearly flawless English, Merten used a megaphone to be heard over the sound of his own diesel engine to ask the name of the ship. George Nutter, formerly the chief radio officer on a troopship, and now traveling home on a long-overdue leave, responded. He was acting as commander of Lifeboat 6, in part because he possessed a lifeboat certificate issued by the Board of Trade. His lifeboat was closest to the sub.

Since he recognized the vessel's name from the distress signal, Merten knew his respondent was being truthful. He asked the usual questions about cargo and destination; Nutter, deciding there was nothing to be gained by lying, answered truthfully, except when asked where the captain of the ship was. Because U-boats were known to take ships' masters prisoner, Captain Rogerson had removed and hidden his uniform jacket. Merten was told the captain had gone down with the ship. Then, perhaps recalling the sinking of the *Laconia* nearly two months earlier, he asked if there were any prisoners of war aboard, or if anyone wanted to be taken prisoner. The reply to both questions was no. Satisfied, Merten then shouted through the megaphone that there were many women and children still in the water, and ordered the lifeboats to pick them up.

When Nutter was asked if he knew his position, the Lancaster native said he did not. Merten then told him the nearest land was the island of St. Helena, some 480 miles north-northeast, course zero-zero-five degrees. He then said they were about 1,000 miles from Walvis Bay, and 3,000 from the South

American coast. While not exact, the distances were close enough for them to pick a destination. Later they all agreed on St. Helena.

Perhaps Merten was also thinking about U-156's rescue attempt at the *Laconia* as he looked out on the several hundred people in the water and on lifeboats. He gave another admonishment about fishing women and children out of the water, then in recognition that he believed it was unlikely any of these people would survive, he apologized to them. "Goodnight," he called to the survivors. "Sorry for sinking you."

The U-boat turned away and slipped off into the darkness. It had been nearly one hour since the first torpedo, and it was time to get out of the area in case an Allied ship had also picked up the distress signal. Korvettenkapitän Merten turned away from the dreadful scene, expecting that all left behind would perish, but he was wrong. In fact, he would see many of these survivors again, years after the war had ended.

In the ensuing weeks, as the survivors of the *City of Cairo* attempted to reach St. Helena, their lifeboats became separated. During this time, people in each lifeboat perished from either injuries received during the attack, or the privations of the elements. The British merchant ship *Clan Alpine* recovered 154 people, including Captain Rogerson and Dulcie and Colin Kendall, and transported them to St. Helena. Another British vessel, the *Bendoran*, found another 47 and took them to Cape Town. Two others, from a lifeboat originally containing 17 people, were rescued on December 27 by the Brazilian corvette *Caravelas* and brought to the *City of Cairo's* original destination, Recife. Three others were picked up by a passing German blockade runner returning to Europe from Japan, named the *Rhakotis*.

The *City of Cairo's* third officer, James A. Whyte, was one of the two survivors picked up by the Brazilian warship. The other was Margaret Gordon. After recovering from their ordeal, they were flown first to Miami, then eventually to New York City. Mrs. Gordon had had enough of the sea, and refused to travel back to England until the war was over. Whyte, looking forward to an appointment as a ship's master, took passage on the *City of Pretoria*, which sailed in convoy from New York for Holyhead, England, with a cargo of ammunition. On March 4, 1943, the *City of Pretoria* was torpedoed by U-172. It sank with total loss of life, including James Whyte.

One of the three people recovered by the German blockade runner died after an emergency tracheotomy performed by the ship's medical officer. The remaining two survived the sinking of the *Rhakotis* by a British warship. One was among the survivors picked up by a U-boat and taken to France. The other was in a lifeboat that eventually landed in neutral Spain.

Despite the inherent dangers, and in contravention of their commander's explicit instructions, some U-boat skippers continued to assist the survivors of ships they had sunk.

Among them were Korvettenkapitän Helmut Witt of U-159, Korvettenkapitän Rudolf Schendel of U-134, and Korvettenkapitän Robert Gysae of U-177.

On the morning of November 13, 1942, two months after the *Laconia* incident, Witt's U-159 fired about 30 shells into the 2,290-ton six-masted steel-hulled American schooner *Star of Scotland* from about two miles off the ship's port beam. The ship was sailing from Cape Town to Brazil, carrying 800 tons of sand as ballast. Knowing his ship was unarmed and without escort, the ship's master, Constantin Flink, quickly ordered the sails struck and the ship abandoned. Sixteen members of the 17-member crew made it safely into two lifeboats, but the chief mate fell overboard while launching one of the two lifeboats aboard the schooner. When the U-boat pulled alongside the lifeboats and inquired of their condition, Witt was informed that one man had fallen into the water and had not been found. For the next two hours the submarine searched the area, with one lifeboat in tow, but failed to locate the man.

Witt was going to take Captain Flink prisoner, so he was brought aboard the submarine. When the merchant seaman explained to the U-boat commander that he was the only member of the crew able to navigate the lifeboats to the African coast some 1,000 miles to the east, Witt asked him to promise not to sail another ship against Germany. Having promised, Flink was returned to his lifeboat. The men were then given some supplies, including tins of black bread and cigarettes, to aid them on their way.

On December 1, the 16 survivors of the *Star of Scotland* landed safely on the Angolan coast, ending a voyage of 1,040 miles. Captain Flink went to great effort to locate Korvettenkapitän Witt after the war and thank him for his kindness.

The day after the *Star of Scotland* was sunk, Korvettenkapitän Rudolf Schendel's U-134 tracked the Panamanian-registered United States–owned 4,827-ton armed steamship *Scapa Flow* several hundred miles to the north. Sailing without escort, the *Scapa Flow* was heading from Freetown to several ports in the Caribbean and ultimately Philadelphia. She was carrying 4,500 tons of manganese ore, 1,500 tons of latex stored in drums, and 500 tons of baled rubber. The ship was hit by two torpedoes and went down within minutes, taking with her the master, Samuel Newbold, and 31 other members of the 60-man crew. Unable to launch the regular lifeboats, the crew did manage to get several rafts and a recently acquired metal boat into the water.

The U-boat approached and asked the usual questions. They gave the men a tin of bandages and what little food they could spare. The Germans told the sailors the direction of the African coast, and bade them good luck as they departed. On December 1, the boats were picked up by the passing British corvette HMS *Armeria*.

Korvettenkapitän Robert Gysae is considered one of the top U-boat aces of the war. From March 27, 1941, through August 1943, he sank 25 ships, including an auxiliary warship, and severely damaged another. On Saturday morning, November 29, 1942, Gysae's U-177 fired three torpedoes at what appeared to be a passenger ship or troopship off the east coast of

South Africa in the Indian Ocean. The ship was the *Nova Scotia*, weighing 6,796 tons and operated by the British government. Formerly a passenger liner, she had been taken over by the Ministry of War Transport in 1941 and converted for use as a troop transport. She sank within minutes of being hit. When the U-boat moved among the survivors and attempted to learn the ship's identity, two men who spoke Italian were fished out of the water. They explained to the U-boat commander that in addition to carrying other passengers, the ship was being used to transport Italian civilian detainees.

The *Nova Scotia* had in excess of 1,000 people aboard when she was attacked. They included 765 Italian civilians, mostly from the former Italian colony of Eritrea, and 134 South African service members on leave from the fighting in North Africa. The rest were crew members or guards for the prisoners, with a smattering of passengers.

When Gysae realized what he had on his hands, his first thoughts must have been similar to Hartenstein's after the *Laconia's* sinking. He decided to get away from the area and seek advice from U-boat headquarters in France. As he departed, the English-speaking survivors could hear him calling out repeatedly in English, "I am sorry. . . . I am terribly sorry. . . . I will radio Berlin. . . . Help will be sent. . . . Be brave."

Headquarters instructed him to resume his patrol, saying that they would arrange for rescue of the survivors. Help was sent in the form of a Portuguese frigate that managed to rescue 194 people. As a direct result of the attack or due to the shark-infected water, 858 people perished. The sinking of the *Nova Scotia* is still considered by many South African historians to be the worst sea disaster in South African waters.

The year 1943 saw a decline in the number of U-boats providing some sort of assistance to survivors. Many factors caused this, most resulting from the January Casablanca Conference between the Allies in which defeat of the U-boats was seen as the "first charge on the resources of the United Nations." More and better aircraft were being used in Anti-Submarine Warfare (ASW), and the Americans had built and deployed their escort carriers, enabling Allied aircraft to cover more ocean territory than if flying from land. The losses among U-boats clearly reveal the difference from one year to the next. In 1942, 85 U-boats were sunk, compared with 237 in 1943. The same month as the Casablanca Conference—January 1943—four U-boats were lost. An RAF aircraft in the North Atlantic sank one. Two others were sent to their doom by American aircraft flying off the Brazilian coast in the South Atlantic.

Whether working as part of a convoy or sailing singly in company with destroyers as submarine hunter-killer groups, the escort carriers proved to be a potent weapon against the U-boats because of their ability to put aircraft in the sky over waters distant from land bases. There was probably nothing as terrifying to surfaced submarine crews as the sudden arrival of enemy planes in the middle of the ocean where they were least expected.

During one 98-day period, three of these small carriers—the USS *Card*, the USS *Core*, and the USS *Bogue*—accounted for the sinking of 24 U-boats. These included 16 attack boats and 8 Milch Cows.

As the number of U-boats destroyed increased dramatically, the number of Allied ships sent to the bottom by submarines dropped precipitously. In the three months from June through August 1943, U-boats accounted for 58 merchant ships sunk, while 79 U-boats were sunk. Of the latter, 58 were destroyed by aircraft.

Yet, in spite of the collapsing world around them, and the tremendously increased danger of disobeying orders, some U-boat commanders continued to put their humanity first. As commander of U-175, Korvettenkapitän Heinrich Bruns sank 10 merchant ships between September 18, 1942, and January 23, 1943. The last was the 7,177-ton Liberty ship SS *Benjamin Smith*. Owned by the South Atlantic Steamship Company of Savannah, Georgia, the ship was sailing from Charleston to the Ghanaian port of Takoradi with about 8,000 tons of war supplies when a torpedo hit her between the number 1 and 2 holds on the starboard side. The engines stalled and the ship began to list as seawater rushed into the opening. Within a few minutes, she came back to a level position and the crew was able to restart her engines. Despite the explosion, the damage was not serious.

The vessel's master, George W. Johnson, attempted to escape further attack by running a zigzag course, but was only able to get up about 6 knots. The mate rushed to the radio shack to give the ship's position to the radio operator, Joe Nolen, who quickly began sending out the SSS signal and repeating the *Benjamin Smith*'s position.

Twenty minutes later a second torpedo, also fired by U-175, struck the ship just behind the engine room and lower down on the hull. This time Johnson knew his ship was doomed. He immediately sounded the abandon ship signal. This explosion shut down the generators and the power throughout the ship went out. Nolen switched his equipment to emergency battery power and began transmitting an SOS, indicating they were abandoning ship. The entire crew of 66, including 23 members of the Naval Armed Guard, left the ship in three lifeboats and a raft. Bruns brought his sub alongside the raft and asked the usual questions. The men answered truthfully, including that the master was not aboard the raft. Bruns must have assumed he was on the ship when it sank, for he never inquired if the master was in one of the lifeboats. He asked if they had enough provisions or needed any medical assistance, and then gave them the course to the coast. Before departing, U-175 fired a third torpedo, which finally sent the ship down.

The men on the raft transferred to one of the lifeboats. One lifeboat had a motor attached, so it towed the others east. The following day they landed on the coast. No one was lost because of the attack.

By the time Kapitänleutnant Asmus Nicolai Clausen caught sight of the Liberty ship *Richard D. Spaight* sailing alone in the Mozambique Channel on March 10, 1943, he was already an ace. U-182 was his fourth command. Since December 1940 he had sunk 21 ships, including the accidental sinking of a Vichy French submarine.

The steamship he had in his sight that evening was only seven months old. In her holds she had 3,000 tons of steel and concrete; lashed to her deck were 32 drums of engine oil. She had sailed from Eritrea on February 25 and was heading to the South African port of Durban, 350 miles south of her current position. U-182 fired two torpedoes at her. The first hit at hold number 1, the second between holds 2 and 3. The ship immediately turned down by her bow. Her master, Russell Hoover Quynn, sounded the abandon ship signal and the entire company of 42 officers and men and 24 armed guard rushed to the lifeboats. One man was killed in the first explosion, but the remainder got off the burning ship safely. The U-boat moved in closer to the ship and fired about 35 rounds from her deck gun, which eventually sent the vessel to the bottom of the channel.

The U-boat then came alongside the four lifeboats and asked the required questions, to which the survivors answered truthfully. Clausen then offered any medical assistance they required as well as food and water before moving away. All four boats reached shore in the next few days without further loss of life.

Did the Laconia Order, or the bombing of the *Laconia's* rescuers, change the way U-boats treated survivors? Prior to the Order, some U-boat commanders would have remained to help survivors while others would have never given such aid. It depended on the individual commander. After the *Laconia* incident, commanders who normally were inclined to help, perhaps recalling Hartenstein's experience, may have decided not to, fearing a similar fate. It would appear Donitz's Laconia Order did not have a serious impact. If anything did, it was the technological advances of the Allies that gave them superiority on the seas.

One man who could have found the Order of value in his own defense was Kapitänleutnant Heinz-Wilhelm Eck, the only U-boat commander charged with a war crime. Eck was convicted of killing survivors from the Greek ship *Peleus*. When questioned concerning the Order, he claimed his copy of it was locked away in his quarters on the submarine, and that he had not given it a moment's thought. What he did was not because of Donitz's order, but rather for the safety of his boat.

Hartenstein's actions following the sinking of the *Laconia* were unique only in the size of the rescue effort. It may be true, as some have written, that he might have been provoked into action by learning that Italian soldiers were among the passengers of the ship he had just sunk. Yet once the rescue was undertaken, he did not hesitate to aid all passengers and crew, regardless of their nationality or enemy status.

CHAPTER 10

Finale

THE *LACONIA* BOATS

The three German U-boats involved in the *Laconia* rescue mission were lost with their crews before the war ended. The Italian submarine outlived the war by only a few months.

U-156

Werner Hartenstein's U-156 was on her fourth patrol when she sank the *Laconia*. The following week, on September 19, 1942, she sank the *Quebec City*, discussed in the previous chapter. This was her last victim. The patrol officially ended on November 16, 1942, when she entered the submarine base at Lorient.

On January 16, 1943, U-156 set out on her fifth and final patrol. Korvettenkapitän Werner Hartenstein, the man who instigated the *Laconia* rescue mission, was still her commander. Most of the crew for this patrol were the same men who had worked tirelessly to save the lives of the *Laconia* survivors the previous September.

Over the next 52 days, U-156 sent 38 position reports back to headquarters. She sailed south until she was off the coast of West Africa, then headed west toward the shipping lanes that connect the South Atlantic to the Caribbean.

The patrol ended in catastrophe on March 8, 1943, in the Atlantic, about 297 miles east of Barbados. The submarine had surfaced in a highly dangerous area patrolled by American warships and ASW aircraft. With Hartenstein's experience and knowledge of the location, the reason for his

U-boat surfacing in daylight remains a mystery to this day. At 1:10 P.M., a U.S. Navy patrol plane caught sight of U-156. The aircraft was a PBY-5 (Patrol Bomber Consolidated Aircraft Corp. version 5) that had flown out of the naval air station at Trinidad earlier that morning. The PBY was a twin-engine flying boat that used its fuselage as a hull in the water. This particular aircraft was part of Patrol Squadron VP-53, piloted by Lieutenant (jg) John E. Dryden. The plane spotted the submarine from a distance of about eight miles. Keeping the sun behind him, and making use of the few clouds available on an otherwise clear and sunny afternoon, Dryden swept in on his target, evidently unseen and unheard by the Germans.

According to Lieutenant Dryden's after-action report, he had clearly seen a tarpaulin covering the one large gun on the submarine, and several men appeared to be sunbathing on her deck. About one-quarter of a mile from the U-boat, the plane dropped out of the cloud cover at an altitude of 1,500 feet and went into a 45-degree dive. Three hundred yards from the target, the bow turret gunner, J. M. Cleary, opened fire with his 30-caliber machine gun. His first burst struck a member of the sub's crew who had been reclining on the platform just behind the conning tower. The man attempted to get up, but the bullets struck his body and drove him back. He slumped down, apparently dead. A second man standing on the deck was also hit. He threw his arms up in a defensive motion and crashed lifeless to the deck. Cleary believed his final burst actually went down the open hatch on the coning tower into the U-boat. Cleary fired 100 rounds at the sub.

Within seconds, Aviation Machinist Mate J. F. Connelly opened fire with his 50-caliber machine gun from the aircraft's port waist blister. He fired 15 rounds, which he believed landed inside the conning tower. From the plane's tunnel hatch, seaman A. Albert fired 30 rounds from his 30-caliber machine gun. All struck the sub midway between her bow and conning tower.

At an altitude of between 75 and 100 feet, Dryden began to pull out of his dive just as he passed over the sub. At the same time, Dryden and his second pilot, Lieutenant (jg) S. C. Beal, pulled the two manual switches that released a salvo of four Mark 44 depth charges. The bombs were filled with Torpex, which was about 50% more powerful than TNT. Two depth charges hit the water about 15 feet from the sub and just behind her conning tower. Within seconds, U-156 broke apart. Her bow and stern both rose into the air as the shattered center sank into the water. A second explosion either caused by the remaining two depth charges or by something inside the submarine threw debris, smoke, and water some 30 to 40 feet in the air.

As the U-boat slipped beneath the surface, a large oil slick spread out, as did a large amount of white foam. Circling overhead, Dryden and his crew counted 11 men clinging to pieces of the wreckage. Within minutes, all but five disappeared from sight. Lieutenant Beal took a position in the rear of the aircraft that allowed him to take the photographs required by navy regulations.

Following Dryden's instructions, Beal dropped two life rafts to the men in the water. The larger of the two failed to inflate. The five survivors of U-156 quickly seized the viable raft. Three men climbed inside while the other two clung to its sides. A short time later an emergency rations kit was tied to two Mae West life jackets and dropped as near to the raft as possible. It landed about 40 feet from the raft and the Germans rowed their little raft over to it.

As the airplane continued to circle the area, Radio Operator W. F. Land attempted to report the incident, but the high volume of radio traffic combined with atmospheric interference forestalled the transmission for 30 minutes. The men in the water reacted to their enemy's flyovers by waving their arms, encouraging them to land their plane in the water nearby.

The Americans reported that four of the survivors appeared to be in their teens and wore only shorts or bathing trunks. The fifth, who was older than the others, wore a shirt in addition to shorts. They thought he might have been an officer. He seemed considerably older than most of the other crew members. Could it have been Hartenstein, rescuer of *Laconia*, now a survivor himself?

Ninety minutes after the attack, Dryden turned back toward his base to avoid running out of fuel. A search-and-rescue mission was launched, but no trace of the German sailors or the raft was ever found. This leaves the question: What happened to the men who survived the sinking of U-156? It is highly possible that despite the sea anchor preventing the raft from drifting, an ocean current carried the men out to sea, where they eventually succumbed to starvation and thirst. Some believe the men may have been rescued. However, for an event of this nature to go unreported, even years later, is improbable.

In the navy's official analysis of the sinking of U-156, it was noted that on the "outbound leg" of Lieutenant Dryden's mission, he reported seeing two Spanish ships within a few hundred miles of U-156. One was the cargo vessel *Aldecoa Espana*, the other the tanker *Gobeo*. Although officially neutral, the Spanish government was believed by the Allies to be leaning toward the Axis powers, at least until the war turned against Germany and Italy. Some researchers have raised the possibility that either or both of these ships heard the aircraft's report of the U-boat sinking and the location of the survivors. They speculate that the men may have been rescued and dropped off in neutral Argentina. The large German community there could have easily assisted them. Others scoff at this speculation. Regardless, the fate of the five men who initially survived the sinking of Werner Hartenstein's U-156 remains unknown.

U-507

Two months before U-156 was sunk, the U-boat commanded by Korvettenkapitän Harro Schacht, U-507, met a similar end. Schacht had been on his third patrol when he helped Hartenstein at the site of the *Laconia* sinking. After turning over his survivors to the French, he resumed this patrol, but was unsuccessful in finding a further target. On October 12, 1942, U-507 returned to base.

U-507's fourth patrol began on November 28, 1942. During this patrol, she sank three British merchant ships. In December, she sank the 5,154-ton *Oakbank,* and reportedly took the ship's master, James Stewart, prisoner. On January 3, her target was the 3,675-ton *Baron Dechmont* with a cargo of nearly 5,000 tons of coal and coke. Again, the ship's master, Donald MacCallum, was taken prisoner aboard the submarine. Five days later the *Yorkwood* was sent to the bottom and her master, Frank Herbert Fenn, was taken prisoner. All three of these men, and possibly several other crew members from their ships, were on board U-507 when it encountered Lieutenant (jg) Ludwig's PBY Catalina patrol bomber.

Ludwig's flying boat was engaged in convoy protection missions, flying out of several U.S. Naval stations along the Brazilian coast. Their primary assignment was to keep an eye on convoys passing along the coast and watch for enemy submarines. The lieutenant and his crew spent the night of January 12, 1943, at a hotel in Fortaleza. Early the following morning, while they prepared their plane for the day's mission, they received a message from the naval station in Natal that a submarine had been spotted shadowing a convoy. Ludwig was told to search for the sub and take appropriate action against it.

The submarine in question was Schacht's U-507. He had been trailing the convoy waiting to pick off more stragglers. Shortly after dawn, flying at an altitude of 6,000 feet about 330 miles off the Brazilian coast, Ludwig spotted the submarine almost below him. He quickly turned and put his plane into a steep dive, pressing the battle station's alarm at the same time. The plane sped down on the submarine at nearly 200 knots. Someone on the U-boat must have detected the approaching aircraft, for it suddenly began to make an obvious emergency dive. As the plane passed overhead, the entire submarine, other than its conning tower, was below the surface. Ludwig and his second pilot released four depth charges when they were less than 50 feet above their target.

As he pulled up and away from the U-boat, Ludwig looked back and described what he saw as "Niagara Falls turned upside down." A mountain of water rose out of the sea where the submarine had been. Ludwig circled the area briefly, but saw no sign of survivors. He radioed the USS *Omaha,* a cruiser escorting the convoy, with the position of the attack. The cruiser left its station and searched the area, but found no trace of the submarine, its crew, or passengers. Evidently, all were lost. Since there was no evidence of a destroyed submarine, the crew was credited with only damaging an enemy submarine. It was not until after the war and German naval records were reviewed that it was finally acknowledged the bomber had sunk U-507.

Ironically, the destruction of U-507 and the deaths of Harro Schacht and his crew followed two failed encounters with U.S. Navy PBY Catalina patrol planes. On May 9, 1942, an aircraft out of Pensacola Florida Naval Air Station dropped depth charges on them without causing serious damage. The following day another Catalina from the same station attacked the U-boat without success. The third encounter was the fatal one.

U-506

When Kapitänleutnant Erich Wurdemann arrived at the site of the *Laconia* rescue, his U-boat, U-506, was on its third patrol. Wurdemann had begun his naval career in 1933 and transferred from surface vessels to the U-boat service in 1940. By the time he had completed four patrols, he had sunk or damaged 17 ships in 337 days at sea. Sailing from Lorient on July 7, 1943, on its fifth patrol, U-506 encountered the United States Army Air Force's powerful 480th Antisubmarine Group. The group was divided into two squadrons flying B-24 Liberators out of Port Lyautey on the Atlantic coast of French Morocco and had had some success in attacking U-boats off the Spanish and Portuguese coasts.

On July 12, 1943, Lieutenant Ernest Salm of the First Antisubmarine Squadron of the 480th Group was piloting his Liberator some 200 miles northwest of Lisbon. This was his first mission as an aircraft commander. The Liberator was searching for enemy submarines from about 5,600 feet using SC137 10 cm radar, which was undetectable by the Germans. As Salm patrolled his area of responsibility, the radar suddenly picked up what appeared to be a submarine some 13 miles away. The sky was heavily overcast, so the men in the plane could see very little below them. Turning his aircraft toward the suspected target, Salm plunged through the gloom at 240 miles per hour, hoping to catch the submarine by surprise. He succeeded.

Finally clearing the thick clouds at 200 feet above the sea, the Americans spotted the surfaced U-boat about one mile away. They were now some 300 miles off the coast of northwestern Spain, almost parallel to Cape Finisterre. Within seconds of sighting the submarine, the Liberator's gunners opened fire on her, raking her deck and conning tower with tracers.

No one appeared on the deck or in the conning tower although it was likely lookouts stationed in the latter that had jumped down into the U-boat at the sound of the approaching bomber. As the Liberator approached U-506, she dropped seven Mark XI 250-pound depth charges filled with the powerful explosive Torpex. While Salm pushed his aircraft into a virtually vertical turn a mere 100 feet above the ocean's surface his crew watched the explosions straddle the U-boat and break her in half.

The B-24 circled back and slowed its speed considerably to examine the results of the attack. Large bubbles broke through the surface as the submarine vanished, and the area became blanketed with oil and debris.

Continuing a slow, low circle of the area, the Americans counted 15 men in the oily water; some waved for help. They dropped an emergency dinghy and several smoke flares to the survivors. After a few more minutes of circling the area, the Liberator left the scene and reported the incident. Leaving, they could see that seven survivors remained. The rest had probably drowned or succumbed to their injuries.

Three days later British destroyers picked up the surviving six members of the U-506 crew. Erich Wurdemann was not among them.

Comandante Cappellini

The career of this *Marcello*-class submarine was unique. She had the distinction of sailing under the flag of all three Axis powers by the time the war ended. In March 1943, after having sunk five enemy ships for a total of 31,648 tons, the *Comandante Cappellini* had her deck guns removed as part of a new program to convert several submarines into cargo vessels to get important war material through Allied blockades. Surface blockade runners taking vital cargos to and from the Far East were being lost at a high rate and using submarines to move this cargo seemed a plausible solution.

After removing much of her combat-related architecture, such as torpedo tubes, she was renamed the *Acquilla III*. On her first mission as a blockade runner, she carried 95 tons of ammunition, torpedoes, and spare parts for U-boats operating in the Indian Ocean and other material for Japan. She arrived at Saipang on July 9, 1943. The next day she sailed to Singapore.

While in Singapore, the Japanese received news of the Italian armistice and placed the Italian crew under arrest. The vessel was then turned over to German naval authorities who replaced some of the guns and renamed her UIT-24. Unable to return to Europe, she was assigned duties in the Southeast Asia theatre for the following year. While in the Mitsubishi Shipyard at Kobe, Japan, news of the German surrender resulted in her confiscation by the Imperial Japanese Navy. Once again, she was given a new name: I-503. As a Japanese submarine, she saw no action. Following the fall of Japan, U.S. Navy ships towed her to sea and sent her to the bottom.

U-162

As for the submarine that had sunk the *Esso Houston* and the skipper who had helped the survivors, their fate was different. In September of the same year, 1942, U-162 came under attack near Trinidad by three British destroyers, HMS *Vimy,* HMS *Pathfinder,* and HMS *Quentin.* After intense bombardment with depth charges, the U-162 was so badly damaged that Kapitänleutnant Wattenberg was forced to surface his boat and order it abandoned just as one of the destroyers rammed her and sent her down. The crew was rescued by the destroyers, except for Engineering Officer

Edgar Stierwaldt, who was below opening the seacocks to scuttle the sub when she went down. Also lost was an enlisted man, Ernst Dettmer, who had a leg injury and likely drowned.

Wattenberg spent the next three years in Allied custody. He became somewhat infamous after leading an escape from Papago Park Prison in Arizona on the night of December 23, 1944. In a classic prison-camp escape using a tunnel dug by the prisoners, 24 German POWs, mostly U-boat officers, followed Wattenberg to freedom, even if only temporarily. The former skipper of U-162 remained free the longest, recaptured on January 28, 1945.

CAPTAIN ROBERT C. RICHARDSON III

The man who gave the order to Lieutenant Harden to attack U-156 during the *Laconia* rescue mission was the son of Robert C. Richardson Jr., the commanding general of the U.S. Army in the Central Pacific for much of the war. Captain Richardson had graduated from West Point in 1939. He trained as a pilot and rose through the ranks as a squadron commander and group operations officer. In April 1942, he was assigned the command of the First Composite Squadron based at Meridian, Mississippi. Richardson and his squadron were redeployed to the top-secret airbase at Ascension Island in June of that year.

In March 1943, Richardson left Ascension Island for a series of assignments that took him from the mainland United States to London, Paris, and finally Germany. In 1949, he was the first Air Force planner for the newly created North Atlantic Treaty Organization (NATO) Standing Group and as such was involved in the German rearmament negotiations. He retired from the Air Force on August 1, 1967, as a brigadier general.

Over the years, controversy over the decision to bomb U-156 had been raised, but Richardson saw no obvious negative impact in his military career or retirement. Reporters and historians attempted to discover why a submarine performing a humanitarian mission, even if it was an enemy, was bombed. That it resulted in the death of a large number of Allied civilians and military personnel made the act even more questionable. Richardson admitted he had given the order to "sink the sub," but said he did not know there were British survivors involved with the U-boat. When questioned about the Red Cross flag draped over the submarine's deck gun, he said he thought it was a trick.

Some people, especially among the *Laconia* survivors, remained bitter against the man who gave the order to bomb them. Several have even charged that his order was a criminal act. However, under the circumstances, Richardson must be given the benefit of the doubt. He was in the middle of an ocean teeming with enemy submarines and one of his aircraft finds a sub with several lifeboats and a Red Cross flag. What did it all mean? Could it have been a trap laying in wait for an Allied ship sent in search of survivors from the *Laconia?* What should one do when an enemy U-boat is discovered on the surface? Could the lifeboats be from a German blockade runner? These may have been some of the questions Richardson and the men on Ascension Island asked themselves. It is very unlikely any considered the possibility that the submarine was giving aid to the survivors of an Allied ship it had sunk.

We need to keep in mind that the base on Ascension was secret. The Americans feared that U-boats would be assigned to attack the supply ships that were its only lifeline if the Germans discovered it. Richardson's primary duty was to use his aircraft to protect the island by seeking out and destroying any enemy submarines found near it. At that point in the war, U-boat crews and commanders were seen as ruthless killers who machine-gunned survivors in the water, not as rescuers. The entire incident and the subsequent events might have turned out differently had Lieutenant Harden or a member of his crew been trained to read the Morse code signals sent to him by U-156. The fact they could not had nothing to do with Richardson. The men of that B-24 were not trained by him, and were not actually a part of his command. There appears to be no resolution to the question of Richardson's culpability. Those who hold him responsible will continue to do so, while others attribute what happened to the "fog of war" and the absence of clear information on which to act.

ADMIRAL KARL DONITZ

As Adolf Hitler prepared for his own suicide, he appointed Admiral Donitz his successor as president. He also gave Josef Goebbels the title of Chancellor. Goebbels was not interested in living after Hitler's death and followed with his own suicide. This left the admiral as the sole ruler of Germany, so it was up to Donitz to accept the surrender terms of the Allies.

Along with most surviving members of the Nazi regime the Allies could find, Donitz faced a series of criminal charges before the International Military Tribunal, more commonly called the Nuremberg War Crimes Trials. What his defense attorney called the "centerpiece" of the charges against Donitz was that through several orders, especially the Laconia Order, he had instructed his U-boat commanders to slaughter survivors of ships they sank. Donitz himself was mortified when he learned of this charge.

When the charge became widely known, 67 former U-boat commanders being held at the POW camp near Featherstone Park, in England, signed a declaration they sent to the tribunal. The document stated "under oath that Admiral Donitz had never given any such orders either orally or in writing."

The defense also introduced sworn testimony from Fleet Admiral Chester Nimitz, who was commander-in-chief of the U.S. Pacific Fleet throughout the war. Nimitz attested to the fact it was "customary" for United States submarines to attack Japanese merchant ships without warning, and in fact had been ordered to do so by the chief of naval operations on December 7, 1941. Nimitz referred to it as "unrestricted submarine warfare." When it came to survivors of ships they had sunk, the admiral stated quite clearly, "On general principles, U.S. submarines did not rescue enemy survivors if undue additional hazard to the submarine resulted or the submarine would thereby be prevented from accomplishing its mission."

Admiral Donitz was indicted on four counts, several of which rested on the charge that he waged an aggressive war by ordering his submarines to attack enemy merchant ships without warning and ordered the U-boat crews to kill survivors in the water. The latter was the key to his expected conviction. However, to the surprise of many, he was found guilty on only two counts and sentenced to 10 years in prison, the shortest term of any of the defendants found guilty by the tribunal. On the most important question of killing shipwrecked survivors, the tribunal stated that it "is of the opinion that the evidence does not establish with the certainty required that Donitz deliberately ordered the killing of shipwrecked survivors."

The conviction of Admiral Dosnitz continues to arouse strong feelings among people of many nationalities and backgrounds. It has been charged that his conviction was for properly training his men to fight in a war— thus the charge that he "waged an aggressive war." Many also feel that he was imprisoned because he was the last German head of state and that he had to be punished for that. It is said he received hundreds of letters of support from admirals, generals, and historians from Allied nations, most expressing their sympathy over his conviction and what many saw as its injustice.

Donitz served his sentence, and on his release went to work on his memoirs. They were published and became a best seller in many countries. By the time of his death in December 1980, at age 89, his reputation was rehabilitated to the point where not only German naval officers attended his funeral, but a number from Allied nations as well.

Bibliography

BOOKS AND ARTICLES

Barker, Ralph. *Goodnight, Sorry for Sinking You: The Story of the S.S.* City of Cairo, London: William Collins Sons and Co., 1984.

Bekker, C. D. *Swastika at Sea: The Struggle and Destruction of the German Navy, 1939–1945.* London: William Kimber, 1953.

Benedetto, William R. *Sailing into the Abyss: The True Story of Extreme Heroism on the High Seas.* New York: Citadel Press, 2005.

Bennett, G. H., and R. Bennett. *Survivors: British Merchant Seamen in the Second World War.* London: The Hambledon Press, 1999.

Berry, Lt. Bob, as told to Lloyd Wendt. *Gunners Get Glory, Lt. Bob Berry's Story of the Navy's Armed Guard.* New York: Bobbs-Merrill Company, 1943.

Blair, Clay. *Hitler's U-Boat War: The Hunted, 1942–1945.* New York: Random House, 1998.

Blair, Clay. *Hitler's U-Boat War: The Hunters, 1939–1942.* New York: Random House, 1996.

Borghese, J. Valerio. *Sea Devils.* Chicago: Henry Regnery Company, 1954.

Bragadin, Antonio. *The Italian Navy in World War II.* Annapolis: Naval Institute Press, 1957.

Bridgland, Tony. *Waves of Hate: Naval Atrocities of the Second World War.* Annapolis: Naval Institute Press, 2002.

Burson, Ray H. *When Lago Was Lucky.* Doniphan, Missouri: self-published, 2006.

Cant, Jeff. "Ascension Island." *After the Battle* no. 32, November 1981.

Dew, Lee A. "The Day Hitler Lost the War." *American Legion Magazine*, February, 1978.

Dmitri, Ivan. *Flight to Everywhere.* New York: McGraw-Hill Book Company, 1944.

Dwyer, Ryle. "Ireland's Close Encounter with German U-Boat." *Irish Examiner.com*, December 30, 1999.

Fowle, Barry W., ed. *Builders and Fighters: U.S. Army Engineers in World War II.* Fort Belvoir, Virginia: Office of History, U.S. Army Corps of Engineers, 1992.

Gasaway, E. Blanchard. *Grey Wolf, Grey Sea.* New York: Ballantine Books, 1970.

Gibbs, Archie. *U-Boat Prisoner: The Life Story of a Texas Sailor.* Boston: Houghton Mifflin Company, 1943.

Grossmith, Frederick. *The Sinking of the* Laconia: *A Tragedy in the Battle of the Atlantic.* Stamford, United Kingdom: Paul Watkins, 1994.

Hawkins, Doris M. *Atlantic Torpedo: The Record of 27 Days in an Open Boat Following a U-boat Sinking.* London: Victor Gollancz Ltd., 1943.

Hochstuhl, William C. *German U-Boat 156 Brought War to Aruba February 16, 1942.* Oranjestad, Aruba: Aruba Scholarship Foundation, 2001.

Hood, Jean. *Come Hell and High Water: Extraordinary Stories of Wreck, Terror, and Triumph on the Sea.* Short Hills, New Jersey: Burford Books, 2006.

Irving, David. *The Destruction of Convoy PQ. 17: The Story of a Major Naval Disaster of World War Two and of Its Political Repercussions.* New York: Simon & Schuster, 1968.

Jones, David C. *The Enemy We Killed, My Friend.* Llandysul, Wales: Gomer Press, 1999.

Kemp, Paul. *Underwater Warriors.* London: Cassell & Company, 2000.

Large, Tony. *In Deep and Troubled Waters: The Story of a South African at War Who Survived the Sinking of Both HMS* Cornwall *and the Troopship* Laconia *in 1942.* Donington, United Kingdom: Paul Watkins, 2001.

Liddell Hart, B. H. *History of the Second World War.* New York: G. P. Putnam's Sons, 1970.

London Evening News. "U-Boat in Irish Port: R.A.F Hunt, Submarine Lands Torpedoed Ship's Crew and Escapes." *London Evening News*, October 5, 1939.

Maurer, Dr. Maurer, and Lawrence J. Paszek. "Origins of the Laconia Order." In *2007 Submarine Almanac*, ed. Neal Stevens. Houston: Deep Domain, 2006.

McLoughlin, Jim, with David Gibb. *One Common Enemy: The Laconia Incident: A Survivor's Memoir.* Kent Town, South Australia: Wakefield Press, 2006.

Moore, John Hammond. *The Faust-Ball Tunnel: German POWs in America and Their Great Escape.* New York: Random House, 1978.

Mulligan, Timothy P. *Neither Sharks Nor Wolves: The Men of Nazi Germany's U-Boat Arm, 1939–1945.* Annapolis: Naval Institute Press, 1999.

Peillard, Leonce. *The Laconia Affair.* Trans. Oliver Coburn. New York: Bantam Books, 1983.

Piekalkiewicz, Janusz. *Sea War 1939–1945.* Trans. Peter Spurgeon. Dorset, United Kingdom: Blandford Press, 1987.

Raithel, Jr., USN, Captain Albert L. "Patrol Aviation in the Atlantic in World War II." *Naval Aviation News*, November–December, 1994, pp. 28–35.

Runyan, Timothy J., and Jan M. Copes, eds. *To Die Gallantly: The Battle of the Atlantic.* Boulder, Colorado: Westview Press, 1994.

Savas, Theodore P., ed. *Silent Hunters: German U-Boat Commanders in World War II.* Campbell, California: Savas Publishing Company, 1997.

Showell, Jak Mallmann. *Fuehrer Conferences on Naval Affairs 1939–1945.* Annapolis: Naval Institute Press, 1990.

Showell, Jak Mallmann. *Wolfpacks at War: The U-Boat Experience in World War II.* Surrey, United Kingdom: Ian Allan Publishing, 2002.

Smith, Jr., Myron J. *World War II at Sea: A Bibliography of Sources in English.* Metuchen, New Jersey: The Scarecrow Press, 1976.

Snyder, Louis L. *Louis L. Snyder's Historical Guide to World War II.* Westport, Connecticut: Greenwood Press, 1982.

Standard Oil Company (New Jersey). *Ships of the Esso Fleet in World War II.* New York: Standard Oil Company (New Jersey), 1946.

Stern, Robert C. *Battle Beneath the Waves: The U-Boat War.* London: Arms and Armour, 1999.

Stern, Robert C. *U-Boats in Action.* Carrollton, Texas: Squadron/Signal Publications, 1977.

Terraine, John. *The U-Boat War, 1916–1945.* New York: G. P. Putnam's Sons, 1989.

Vause, Jordan. *Wolf: U-Boat Commanders in World War II.* Annapolis: Naval Institute Press, 1997.

Von der Porten, Edward P. *The German Navy in World War II.* New York: Galahad Books, 1969.

Wiggins, Melanie. *U-Boat Adventures: Firsthand Accounts from World War II.* Annapolis: Naval Institute Press, 1999.

Zabecki, David T. *Donitz: A Defense.* Bennington, Vermont: Merriam Press, 2003.

VIDEO

A & E Television Networks. *The Laconia Incident.* New York: New Video, 1997.

WEB SITES

Armed-Guard.com. "World War II U.S. Navy Armed Guard and World War II U.S. Merchant Marine." http://www.armed-guard.com.

ConvoyWeb. "The Website for Merchant Ships during World War II." http://www.convoyweb.org.uk.

"Deutsch U-Boote 1935–1945." U-Boat History (German). http://www.u-boot-archiv.de.

HyperWar Foundation. "A Hypertext History of the Second World War." http://www.ibiblio.org/hyperwar.

Kosour, Ladislav. "Warships of World War II." http://www.warshipsww2.eu.

Lago Oil & Transport Co., Ltd. "Lago Colony and Lago Refinery, Aruba." http://www.lago-colony.com.

The Nizkor Project. "The International Military Tribunal: Nuremberg." http://www.nizkor.org/hweb/imt/.

PBY.com. PBY Aircraft. http://www.pby.com.

Regiamarina. "Italian Submarines in World War II." http://www.regiamarina.net/subs.

Sixtant. "War II in the South Atlantic." http://sixtant.net.

"SS *City of Cairo*." http://www.sscityofcairo.co.uk.

U-35.com. U-35 History. http://www.u-35.com.

U-Boat Archive. http://www.uboatarchive.net.

Uboataces.com. "German U-Boats and Battle of the Atlantic." http://www.uboataces.com.

Uboat.net. "The U-Boat War 1939–1945." http://www.uboat.net.

Ubootwaffe.net. "Kriegsmarine and U-Boat History." http://www.ubootwaffe.net.

U.S. Merchant Marines. "American Merchant Marine at War." http://www.usmm.org.

USAAF.net. "The United States Army Air Forces in World War II." http://www.usaaf.net/.

Vpnavy.org. "U.S. Navy Patrol Squadrons." http://www.vpnavy.org.

Warsailors.com. Norwegian Merchant Fleet in World War II. http://www.warsailors.com.

"Werner Hartenstein." http://wernerhartenstein.tripod.com.

WW2 People's War: http://www.bbc.co.uk/ww2peopleswar/.

Index

CPSIA information can be obtained at www.ICGtesting.com
Printed in the USA
BVOW030004120213

312970BV00002B/2/P